Food and Freedom

Gabriella Lang

Copyright © Gabriella Lang, 2022

Published: 2022 by The Book Reality Experience
Leschenault, Western Australia
****

ISBN: 9781922670724 – Paperback Edition
ISBN: 9781922670731 – E-Book Edition

The right of Gabriella Lang to be identified as author of this work has been asserted by her in accordance with sections 77 and 78 of the copyright, designs and patents act 1988.

This book is a memoir, reflecting the author's present recollections of experiences over time. This means that some details may vary from fact. Some names and characteristics may have been changed, some events have been compressed, and some dialogue has been recreated. Memory can be a fickle thing, so the Author trusts that any minor errors in times, dates and details of particular events will be understood.

All rights reserved. No part of this publication may be reproduced or transmitted in any form or by any means, electronic or mechanical, including photography, recording, or any information storage or retrieval system, without permission in writing from the publisher.

The book is sold subject to the condition that it shall not, by way of trade or otherwise, be lent, resold or otherwise circulated without the publisher's prior consent in any form of binding or cover other than that in which it is published and without a similar condition, including this condition, being imposed on the subsequent purchaser.

Cover Design by Brittany Wilson | Brittwilsonart.com

For Amelia and Angelica
with all my love.

Table of Contents

Food and Freedom 1
Introduction 3
CHAPTER ONE Flags and 'Flemingtons' 10
  Recipe for Flemingtons 17
CHAPTER 2 The Dead House 19
CHAPTER 3 The Bullet List 31
  Recipe for chocolate hazelnut biscuits 43
CHAPTER 4 Echoes 45
CHAPTER 5 My Father's Piano 62
CHAPTER 6 Feasts of Christmas Past 78
  Recipe for Beigli. 89
CHAPTER 7 Student Life 93
CHAPTER 8 The Suitcase 107
CHAPTER 9. Travel Broadens The Mind, The Hips, and The Waistline 123
CHAPTER 10 Liar, Liar. Your Regime Is On Fire! 138
CHAPTER 11 The Diggers' Club 155
  Recipe for Lángos 175
CHAPTER 12 Strudel Wars or Rétes Rivalry 177
  Recipe for Megyes Rétes (sour cherry rétes) 197
CHAPTER 13 When Autumn Leaves Start to Fall 199
CHAPTER 14 Going Home 217
Acknowledgements 241
About the Author 243

Food and Freedom

Our second day in Hungary.

My mother and I stand in the park at the junction of Győr's three rivers. To our left, the industrial area of the city belches smoke but the vista before us is mesmerizingly beautiful. Snow-covered lawns roll down to meet the swirling waters, the frozen trees stand silhouetted along the bank and ice floes drift lazily by. The sky above us is piercing, iridescent blue. A flock of birds rise up from the steeple of the old church and sweep across the sky in a silver ribbon. I turn to my mother and ask, "How could you bear to leave all this beauty?"

Without shifting her gaze, she sighs and answers,

"For food. And for freedom."

Introduction

"If it doesn't feel right, beat it a bit more."

I read these words three more times before admitting defeat.

'Feel right? A bit more?'

What does that mean? What do I do next? I stare down at the mess in the bowl and poke it with my finger. The gooey chocolate clings to it and in a Pavlovian response, I put it into my mouth. To my amazement, it is rich, nutty and delicious. It may not look 'right', but it tastes wonderful.

Ignoring the rest of the cryptic instructions, I roll out the sticky mixture, cut it into small rounds and slide them onto the baking tray. Shoving the whole thing into the hot oven, I settle back to wait.

Ten minutes later, a wonderful rich aroma fills the kitchen. But when I peer into the oven, I see that each perfect little disk has disintegrated, crumbling into a molten, ugly heap. I yank the tray out and burn my hand as I plonk it unceremoniously onto the bench. I burst into tears.

I need my mother.

I really, really need my mother.

This is her recipe. This is her kitchen and I need her to help me.

But she can't. She is lying in bed, trying to summon the strength to get up and see the visitors who are due any minute. My mother is dying of cancer. But for once, it's not the tragedy of that precious life fading away that unhinges me – it's the gooey mess on the bench. Further evidence – not that any was needed – of my many failings as a pastry-chef.

I make myself stop crying. This is not the end of the world. My mother's friends are coming to see her; they are not coming to eat biscuits. Which is just as well because I don't have any biscuits to offer them.

Unlike last week. And recalling that particular debacle, I burst into tears again.

Despite all my efforts to do the right thing, the visit last week had been an unmitigated disaster. I tried so hard to make it seem as if everything was fine, but the plate of store-bought *Choc Gourmet Cookies* had, more than anything, brought home to everyone just how far from 'fine' things were.

The visit started well. Three couples arrived together, driving their cars in convoy as they had always done. They greeted me and hugged me all the while talked very loudly in Hungarian and for a precious moment I was transported back into my childhood, gathered into the love of these dear people whom I had known most of my life. Before they came, I had been dreading it – my emotions now so raw that the thought of seeing them was almost more than I could cope with. But now they were here my spirits lifted.

As well as love, they brought masses of flowers with them and if they were shocked at the terrible toll cancer had wrought on my mother's appearance, they hid it well. They embraced her long and tenderly – even the men. None of that stiff upper lip nonsense for these old friends. They held her close and soon the room was filled with the scent of blossom and the sound of laughter and chatter. Like it had been hundreds, maybe thousands of times over the years.

Then, just as I was starting to relax and enjoy myself, it unravelled in spectacular fashion. I went into the kitchen to make coffee – the aromatic strong brew that even after 50 years in Australia they had not abandoned in favour of a less lethal beverage. But as I set the tray with the dainty cups and saucers my mother always used, I suddenly realised that I had no biscuits or pastries to accompany the coffee. Disaster!

Such a thing was unheard of in this house. Unprecedented! Unthinkable!

My mother was a magnificent cook. Her dinner parties were legendary and above all, her cakes, biscuits, slices and desserts were things of beauty and delight. Anyone crossing her threshold came assured of a feast, with never less than three different types of sweet delicacies to be savoured, with the rest packed into small foil-covered parcels to take home. And that was just for the unexpected visitor. If the guest had been anticipated, the selection of offerings was dizzying. Years ago, I asked my mother why she didn't just make one dessert or one type of cake for her guests. She looked up from energetically beating egg-whites into submission and said, in a tone that indicated such a thought had never occurred to her, "Just one cake? Are you crazy?"

At this crucial moment however – with the waiting guests assembled in the next room – I would have committed murder for 'just one cake'. Guilt – such a familiar emotion these days – swept over me. I should have thought of this. I should have made sure I had something suitable to offer the guests. No Hungarian woman ever dreamt of bringing food of any kind to a gathering. It was the ultimate insult and implied that the hostess was incapable of producing something mouth-watering. Which, in this particular case, was an accurate assessment of the situation.

Cursing Hungarian customs in general and those involving food in particular, I was about to bring disgrace to my entire family for generations by serving only coffee when I suddenly remembered. Almost slipping over in my haste, I rushed to the pantry and grabbed the packet of biscuits I'd bought last week in a haze of misery-fuelled sugar craving. They looked delicious. I arrange them artistically and carried them in with the coffee, setting the tray down with a flourish.

And there they stayed. Untouched. The coffee quickly disappeared but not one guest so much as looked at the biscuits. For the rest of the visit, the Choc Gourmet Cookies sat on the floral plate, sadly reproaching me with their factory produced symmetry. Unwittingly, I had led the chocolate equivalent of an elephant into the room. The potent symbol of the illness that was taking my mother away from us – something we could all see but no-one could acknowledge.

My mother was growing tired, so the guests left soon afterwards. When I walked everyone to their cars, they gathered around and hugged me. It was time for us all to cry. No words, just the silent acknowledgment of death hovering overhead. As George kissed me goodbye, he said in a voice choked with tears. *"Viszontlátásra, szép kislány!"*

"Goodbye pretty little girl." I had known him most of my life and he always said goodbye to me like this. In another rush of pain, I wondered if I was not only about to lose my mother but with her would go the connection to these dear people and the only remaining link I still retained to my native land.

The cars drove off. I went back inside, carefully replacing the bright smile (idiot grin, more like) I now adopted when I was with my mother. She was sitting where we had left her in her favourite chair by the window. Her eyes were closed and I thought she had fallen asleep. But as I moved towards her, she looked at me and a single tear rolled down her cheek. Gesturing towards the offending biscuits, she said sadly, "I should have baked something!"

***

As a small child, I couldn't understand why the English-speaking world insisted on calling my ancestral home – that proud, ancient land of the Magyars – Hungary. But over the years, I have come to realise that this connection to food is appropriate.

Hungarians love to eat, drink and be merry. But even more – or so it has always seemed to me – they love to feed others. Hospitality is a way of life for them and if you're ever lucky enough to be invited over for a meal, you will not remain 'hungry' for long. In fact, you don't even have to be invited over for a meal – any person crossing a Hungarian woman's threshold for any, or indeed no, particular reason is immediately seen as a prime candidate for feeding.

I grew up in a household where superb food was the order of the day. The fact that as a child I was a finicky eater was not viewed as a mild irritation – it presented a major challenge and my mother and grandmother vied with each other to prepare meals I would deign to eat. The competition was fierce at times.

Both women were inventive cooks. My mother especially lived and breathed the belief that 'food is love', although she didn't have to actually love someone to feed them. She really believed that all the major ills of the world could be alleviated by a delicious meal and fine wine. Especially if the meal ended with copious amounts of 'something sweet'.

My mother was the person we all turned to when the world threw us a curve ball. Not just her own family but myriad friends and neighbours would go to her for comfort, wisdom and cake, though not necessarily in that order.

There is lovely joke about a (fill in nationality, but I'll bet you it was originally Hungarian) mother during a war. Her only son is away fighting the enemy and she stands by the gate every day anxiously awaiting his return. Finally, after many months, she sees him in the distance. He staggers up the path and falls into her arms, blood pouring from his many wounds.

"Mother!" he gasps, barely alive.

"Hush," she admonishes. "Eat first. Talk later!"

And that was how it was for all of us. No problem was too great that several pieces of cake, biscuit or slice would not make it better. Sometimes, if you ate enough, the problem went away altogether.

I never really knew my mother, although I only realised this after she died. As a child, I was too busy trying to work out who I was becoming to care who she was. After my daughter was born and my relationship with my mother improved dramatically, my perception of her was still as my mother and Amelia's adored grandmother. I saw her not for who she was, but who I was in relation to her.

Then she died. I found her letters and notebooks and gradually, I began to get some glimpse of the real her – the person behind the persona. And the places and influences that shaped her. Who she had once been, who she had ultimately become and the journey that took her there.

This new perception stunned me out of my grief; grief that as time passed became sharper rather than diminished. The mother I thought I knew had been practical, organised, not given to sentiment. I did not know this woman whose words I now read. Words written only a few years ago while on a train travelling back from her childhood village in Hungary to the city where she was staying with relatives. Describing the old walnut tree in her parent's garden, she admitted it made her weep at memories of her childhood. And she wrote about the agonising decision she made many years ago to leave her old life behind and how – even after all this time – her Hungarian homeland still tugged at her heart.

'We have cockatoos, such brightly coloured and happy birds in the garden in Sydney. So different to here. But last night, the owl's cries almost broke my heart. Gum trees for walnut trees and kookaburras for swallows. This is the choice I made then. And this is the choice I would make again. But it breaks my heart…'

I knew she loved my father – his sudden death five years before her own devastated her. But I had no idea of the depth of her pain until I read in her notebook on the third anniversary of his passing -*'My darling! I still miss you so!'*

Such passionate words from a woman who appeared to scorn sentiment. Whose advice in the face of adversity had always been, "Pull yourself together and get on with it!" And taking her own words to heart when my father died, she got on with life, burying her grief deep inside.

CHAPTER ONE
Flags and 'Flemingtons'

My parents escaped from Hungary in November 1956. A newly married young couple caught up in the desperate exodus of mainly young professional people who voted with their feet when the Russian tanks rolled into Hungary and the killing spree began.

Like most of those brave refugees, my mother and father had no choice but to walk through the countryside to the Austrian border. As a child, I never appreciated how terrifying an ordeal this must have been and it is only now that I look back on their adventure with a mixture of incredulity and great admiration. They walked for 60km – across muddy frozen fields at night, while by day they hid in undergrowth from the patrolling Russian troops who had orders to shoot on sight. Every step took them further away from family, friends and the life they knew, but they were young and idealistic and somehow after three gruelling days, they made it to the border.

Many years later, hearing about a marriage that had come apart at the seams and the couple were separating, my mother looked stunned and asked why. When she was told that 'the spark had gone' she shook her head before declaring, "The sparkle went out of my marriage on the Hungarian border when your father and I were being shot at by Russians. But we stayed together!"

Yes, they stayed together and over the next 50 years built a marriage of great love, commitment and faith.

It must have been very difficult in the beginning. After three desolate months in a refugee camp in Melk in Austria, my parents arrived in Sydney – a place so completely alien to them that they felt they had been transported to another planet. Hand in hand, they looked around nervously and waited to see if the natives were friendly. They were. Friendly, welcoming and warm. Australia took the young couple into their hearts and in return, my parents came to passionately love their new homeland.

Had Australia ever been threatened by a foreign aggressor, I feel sure that my father would have taken up arms in defence of his adopted country. And done it well – in his youth, he had been a crack rifle shot. And my mother would no doubt have volunteered for the catering corps, thus contributing significantly to the quantity and even more to the quality of the food.

Fortunately, it never came to this. But every year, my mother took great delight in honouring Australia's armed forces on ANZAC Day. In a fanfare of flags and Flemingtons.

Without fail, every 24th of April, out came the Australian Flag from its home under the stairs. My mother inspected it carefully and when it passed muster, she instructed my father to erect the flagpole in the front garden ready for the flag to fly proudly all the next day. When we were teenagers, my brother and I hated this ritual with a passion. It was irrelevant that the flag was not really all that big and the flagpole only made a brief annual appearance. We found the entire performance mortifying.

As everyone knows, rain on ANZAC Day is as much part of tradition as floppy digger hats. Or the game my mother insisted on calling Up Two!

On one occasion, I was thrilled when my mother discovered that the flag was covered in mould after having been put away damp the previous year. I rejoiced, thinking we were to be saved from our ritual embarrassment but I had reckoned without my mother's determination. My long-suffering father was dispatched into Manly with instructions not to come home flagless. I remained optimistic for a while longer – it was almost 5pm by this stage and surely all the shops had shut?

But in an hour or so, he arrived home carrying a – smaller than I'm sure my mother had hoped – flag. He swept into the kitchen waving it triumphantly, looking for all the world like a middle-aged revolutionary manning the barricades. My mother rewarded him with a hug and a slice of cake while I sat on the stairs and wished – not for the first time – I had never been born.

Every ANZAC Day my mother and often my father, would get up at 4am and attend the Dawn Service in Manly. As soon as they got home, up went the flag, on went the television and down went my mother – onto the couch where she stayed and watched the ANZAC Day March. The entire March. Four and a half hours of March. Fuelled by cups of coffee and various snacks, she sat through it all and become so familiar with many of the marchers year after year that if someone distinctive was missing, she noticed. "The man with the crutch and funny ears isn't here this year. Poor thing. I hope he is ok?"

One year – I think I was sixteen – driven to despair with embarrassment (my mother had managed get her hands on a *really* big flag, so big you could hear it flapping outside in the wind!) I sat down next to my mother. As she watched the ex-

Diggers parade past, I politely pointed out that it was not outside the realms of possibility that some of those aging soldiers, whom she was cheering so enthusiastically, had been shooting at Hungarians during the Second World War. At her father or uncles possibly? "We were on opposing sides you know," I added helpfully, really trying to drive the point home.

My mother turned and glared at me. She was silent for as long as it took for me to feel ashamed of myself – which I blush to admit, was longer than it should have been. Then she said quietly, "It doesn't matter. They were young. And brave. And they fought for their country."

Says it all really, doesn't it?

My father – while every bit as patriotic – was more pragmatic. When I asked him one year why he attended the Dawn Service, he smiled his slow smile and said, "Hungarians are used to celebrating spectacularly disastrous military operations!"

He had a point. Even a cursory reading of European history illustrates two facts; firstly, that Hungarians always – without exception – manage to end up fighting on the losing side in an armed conflict. I don't know how they do it but faced with two opposing factions – say the Triple Entente and the Triple Alliance in the early 20th century, or the Nazis and the Allies 25 year later, yes, you guessed it – losing side. Every. Single. Time. Well, mostly. I'm not actually a scholar of military history. But I do know that secondly – every medium to large European nation worth its salt has conquered Hungary. Some conquests were relatively short-lived because the conquerors were actually on their way to rape, pillage and plunder some other country and Hungary seemed like a really pleasant place to stop off for lunch. While others – yes USSR, I'm talking about you! – lasted for almost half a century. But my personal favourite long occupation was by the Ottoman Empire. The Turks came, saw, conquered and then forgot to leave for a hundred and fifty years. By the time they did eventually decamp, having being been forced out by the Austrians, they left an enduring legacy of onion-domed churches, beautiful dark-eyed women and excellent coffee.

Yes, the history of my homeland makes sad reading. It has however contributed to the Hungarian sense of humour. In spite of their tragic history, the endless bloodshed, wars, revolutions – you name it – Hungarians are able to laugh at themselves and make light of the most appalling situations.

They are also excellent at bearing grudges. I remember my grandfather once being less than complimentary about the Serbs. When I asked him why he didn't like them, he answered, "The Battle of Mohacs!" This skirmish took place in **1427** so it may not have been inappropriate to suggest the time had come to move on.

Hungary is a small country although if you meet a group of Hungarians you would be tempted to think it sounds larger. But it wasn't always small. As part of the Austro-Hungarian Empire in the 19th century, it had a land mass of some 330,000 square kilometres and was a significant player on the European stage. Unfortunately, this ended in 1920 when – as retribution for being on the (you guessed it) losing side during World War I, it lost over 70% of its territory. The carve-up of the country by the victorious French and English occurred at the Treaty of Trianon. A disaster from start to finish, this laid the groundwork for the inevitable ethnic conflicts that flared over the next 90 year in places such as Kosovo and Sarajevo.

Let's be frank here – having not been properly planned beforehand, Trianon was never, ever going to be a raging success. The English representative – Edward Villiars, Earl of Derby – fronted up to the negotiating table less than 100 percent clear about the exact geographical location of Hungary – the country he was about to dismember. Although an atlas was hastily produced and the oversight rectified, it did less than nothing to give the Earl a better understanding of these centuries long ethnic diversities and conflicts. Yes, I'm sure that after four and a half bloody years of war, everyone was a wee bit tired and emotional. And yes, dismembering counties must be really hard work. But in my humble opinion, Trianon was *not* England's finest hour.

Most Hungarians agreed. When I was 18, I told my grandfather about a very nice young lad I had just met at university. When I added that he was English, my grandfather looked troubled. "English! Not to be trusted!" he warned.

"Why?" I asked.

"Trianon!" he answered, shaking his head sadly.

No Hungarian celebration is complete without food so as well as flag-flying and ritual mortification of teenage children, when I was growing up, ANZAC Day included cake. 'Flemingtons' to be exact, although to most people they looked a lot like Lamingtons. When my mother was first introduced to this Aussie icon soon after her arrival here, she thought they bore the name of the Sydney suburb. By the time she discovered her mistake, the name had stuck.

She not only rechristened the delicacy, she improved it. My mother's Flemingtons contained two layers of vanilla sponge, joined together with strawberry jam, rolled in a double layer of dark chocolate and toasted coconut. I have no idea if it was any one of these innovations that lifted her cake from the delicious to the sublime or a combination of them all but they were mouth-watering. And meant for sharing. So, every 24th April between flag inspecting and flagpole erecting, my mother found time to bake tray after tray. She arranged these on six special plates (only ever used on this day, they featured cringe-inducing paintings of Australian flora and fauna) and distributed them to the neighbours, who had all been eagerly anticipating this treat since early morning. Every local cook asked for the recipe and many tried to replicate it but somehow, their efforts were never quite as good as hers.

I baked my first batch of Flemingtons on ANZAC Day a month after my mother died. I carefully placed them on two plates decorated with kangaroos and koalas. Then – without really intending to – I sat down and watched the March. And I cried. For those brave old Diggers. For the loss of young lives in so many conflicts. But most of all, for that dear woman who had taken such a truly Australian celebration and made it her very own.

1957. Otto and Helen visiting the Blue Mountains for the first time

Recipe for Flemingtons

Ingredients:

1 square or rectangular vanilla sponge cake, at least one day old. Fresh cake will disintegrate into a gooey mess so don't even bother.

4 cups icing sugar- very well sifted

5 tablespoons Dutch cocoa

4 tablespoons unsalted butter

2 tablespoons boiling water

3 cups shredded coconut

Strawberry jam

Method:

- Cut cake into equal size cubes. Then cut each piece in half (so it can be filled with jam). Freeze for at last an hour. 90 minutes if possible.

- Spread each half piece with strawberry jam. Sandwich together.

- Meanwhile, make the chocolate icing. Melt half the butter in a saucepan. Add half the cocoa and half the icing sugar. Stir until smooth. Add tablespoon or so of boiling water if needed. It should be thick enough to coat the back of a spoon.

- Carefully dip each cube of cake in melted chocolate until completely covered. Put back in freezer again for at least 30 minutes.

- Meanwhile, toast the coconut on a large tray in the oven. On 170C. Should take about 10 minutes but be careful - it can burn easily. Cool.

- Make the rest of the chocolate icing as before.

- Dip each cube of cake again into the melted chocolate and immediately into the toasted, cooled coconut. Press coconut onto surface to make sure you get a good covering.

- Refrigerate – not freeze - for at least 30 minutes.

- Take out of refrigerator at least 30 minutes before serving.

- Can be served with whipped cream. And best eaten while watching the ANZAC Day March.

CHAPTER 2
The Dead House

It only took my parents twelve months to save up enough money to buy their first home after settling in Sydney. I don't know how they did it on their meagre salaries, but lots of overtime was involved and new clothes didn't feature in their lives. But whatever sacrifices they had to make, it was worth it.

As if by magic, at just the right moment the perfect house appeared. Actually, it was very far from perfect – and from the photos I've seen, it is somewhat of a stretch to call it a house. A huge looming shell covered in ivy, with broken windows and an overgrown front yard partially buried under rubble. Even the real estate agent had qualms about overselling it and described it as a 'Deceased Estate', before adding the blindingly obvious 'Needs Work'.

But if you stood directly in line with the front of the house and contorted your body to the left while kneeling on the pavement (which for some unknown reason my mother happened to be doing one day), you could see the beautiful fanlight above the front door. Having grown up in a house with just such a fanlight, she took this as a good omen. Every morning for four weeks, she visited it either alone or with my father, until the day arrived when they had scraped together the final instalment of the deposit. It was time to see inside.

Neither of my parents had ever bought a house before. In fact, nor had their parents or their grandparents. Back in Hungary both their families had lived in properties passed down through the generations – my father originally in a pretty townhouse in Győr – so pretty that in 1948, a high-ranking officer of the occupying Russian army moved in. The family moved out into a small cottage that had also been in the family for over 100 years. My mother's family owned vineyards, which the Russians also confiscated in 1948 together with the house. They too moved to something much smaller they owned in the same village.

So, buying a house was a big adventure for my parents. They treated the enterprise with the respect it deserved by dressing appropriately – my father in his one suit and my mother in her blue dress and cream jacket. They were very nervous and my father, having been designated spokesperson, had practised his speech. He was going to ask the agent to take them for, "An inspection of the deceased estate on Johnstone Street, Annandale. Please. Thank you."

But words like 'inspect' and 'deceased estate' did not as yet trip lightly off his tongue and he ended up asking to, "Look at the dead house." Which, in the circumstances, was a much more accurate description. Still, the agent got the message, piled them into his car and drove them over. No-one else had been brave or deluded enough to view the property and it took them a while to defeat the ivy that was proving especially tenacious. But finally, they got the front door open and light flooded the interior. Holding hands, my parents walked across the black and white tiles. They didn't notice that every single tile was cracked. Or that the plasterwork was falling off in chunks. They saw sunlight and golden opportunity and their bright future stretching ahead of them down the long hallway.

Rubble and broken floorboards prevented them from going into some of the rooms, but they saw enough to declare, "We buy!" But Mr Tom the agent, instead of rubbing his hands together and rejoicing in his good fortune at offloading this derelict pile to the naïve young couple beaming so happily at him, proved to be a true gentleman. He felt sorry for them, suggested they think about it over the weekend and come back to him on Monday. When he saw their disappointment, he added kindly, "Hang onto the keys until then and have a really good look around." A very generous offer, though not exactly fraught with danger as there was no more damage anyone could possibly inflict on this ruin.

My parents hurried home. Changing out of their good clothes, they collected a few essentials and raced back to the house where for the next hour they wandered around exploring, pushing open doors, forcing open windows and letting in sunlight for the first time in many years. Everything they saw delighted them – the high patterned ceilings, the massive panelled doors between the sitting and dining rooms, even the two bathrooms with enormous – and indescribably filthy – deep baths and tessellated tile floors. The house boasted five bedrooms, several living spaces and a cavernous kitchen with the original *Kookaburra* stove still in situ. Unfortunately, most of the floor wasn't (in situ, that is) and part of the back wall had collapsed. The ivy growing on it had made its way inside and across the ceiling, giving it a creepy Agatha Christie 'murder-in-the-greenhouse' effect.

But on that first day they fell in love with every last crumbling inch. After the past year living in a cramped single room, my father revelled in the high ceilings and the feeling of space. My mother adored the big windows and the configuration of the rooms. It had once been a beautiful house and they knew it could be again. Any remaining doubts they may have had about undertaking such a massive project were dispelled as soon as they went into the back garden. It was enormous, although this was not immediately obvious – it was home to two rusty car chassis, numerous tyres, several large metal crates and a pile of building rubble the size of most inner-city semis.

Beyond the rubbish dump right at the back stood six fruit trees – apple, apricot and pear. They were gnarled and neglected but still recognisable, planted in a circle of lawn with a stone bench – miraculously still intact – in the middle. For several more hours the young couple wandered round, exploring the house and garden to their hearts' content. And then it was time to celebrate. They sat on the grass beneath the fruit trees in the warm November twilight and toasted the house and their new lives together with a half bottle of cheap red wine they had brought for this very purpose.

It is my favourite memory of them. Although I was not present, I've heard the story many times and I've seen enough photos to be able to visualise the scene and them in it. My mother with her hallo of dark curly hair and my father's shy smile. And then there is the part they didn't tell me or not in so many words. But whenever they spoke of this afternoon, my mother blushed and stole a glance at my father. I think – I so hope – they made love there that evening in the overgrown garden, outside the house they would transform into a beautiful home. Beneath the warm Australian sky they were growing to love.

A few short weeks later the house was theirs and the real work began. Initially it was a matter of getting rid of the staggering amounts of rubbish accumulated inside. Helped by a group of loyal friends, they tackled a room at a time, carrying, pushing and shoving the rubbish towards the back of the house out into the back garden. Every week or so, they spent some of their precious cash to hire a large skip to take it all away via the back lane. After six weeks of marathon effort the rubbish was gone, and the house emerged in all its splendour.

It had what might be referred to as 'good bones'. But there was not a skerrick of flesh on them so a lot of money was needed to bring it back to life. Unfortunately, money was the one thing they had run out of by this point in the exercise, but fuelled by the heady mix of first home owners' euphoria and sheer physical exhaustion, they pressed on. What if they had absolutely nothing left in the bank after the purchase? They were blessed with unlimited energy, boundless enthusiasm and *lots* of friends.

Around 20,000 of their countrymen came to Sydney as refugees in 1956. While many of them were middle class professionals, there was also a large contingent of tradesmen. The Hungarian tom-toms went into overdrive and within days a veritable army of bricklayers, plumbers, tilers and carpenters descended on the house. None of these highly skilled craftsmen had yet managed to gain employment in Sydney within their areas of expertise so all the work was done at night and over the weekend. The pointing in the brickwork was meticulously restored by Laslo who worked as a labourer during the day. Joseph did all the plumbing when not waiting tables at the local café and Pal – a true artist – raced home from his job as packer at the glass factory to transform the bathrooms by laying tile mosaics of such beauty and complexity they made you weep.

Supervising this hive of activity (and illegal building work!) my parents went without sleep for the best part of a year. My father did a double shift in the factory six days a week to pay for the materials while my mother worked ten-hour days as a cleaner at the local hospital before coming home to scrub, wash and when the need arose, hold ladders, mix concrete or indulge in a relaxing spot of plastering.

But most of the time, she cooked – vast meals for the workers and for the lodgers. As soon as each bedroom was cleared of rubble, two of the tradesmen moved in. By the end of that year, in addition to my parents there were eight young men occupying the four spare bedrooms. It was a win-win. My parents received a nominal rent plus unlimited manpower while the tenants had somewhere pleasant to live. Although 'pleasant' is rather an overstatement. Initially, they got a room with four walls or possibly three and sections of tarpaulin. But they also got companionship, camaraderie, lots of laughs. And my mother's cooking.

When my mother first embarked on what was to become her passion, she was a novice. At the age of nine, she had been sent to boarding school to be educated by Catholic nuns, who were required to teach the young ladies in their care how to walk, sit, embroider and supervise the preparation – but not the actual cooking – of meals. But remember, this was Hungary – so the girls were also required to turn their hands to the baking of cakes and the preparation of desserts. Unfortunately, all too soon the horror of war put an end to these gentle pastimes and tapestries and menu cards went right off the agenda. By 1943 in Hungary, *food* pretty much went right off the agenda, followed by Catholic nuns and priests once the Russians took control. My mother returned to her family to continue her education as best she could while living through the communist takeover in fear, cold and close to starvation. As landowners, at first her family did not fare quite as badly as their city cousins because they still raised crops and occasionally slaughtered an animal for food. But cooking lessons? Not so much.

The end of the war left Hungary in a terrible state – many of her cities bombed flat and the people beaten down by the brutal conquering Russian army. Eventually the Russians stopped pretending they had liberated the country from the Nazi regime. They took complete control, reducing the proud homeland of Attila to a subservient member of the mighty USSR, a disempowered 'satellite state' of the Soviet Block. Very slowly life improved for the general population but when my parents got married, things were still exceedingly grim. Meals consisted of whatever you could grow, barter or – only occasionally – buy in the understocked food stores. Unsurprisingly, my mother's lessons in cake-making and table decoration remained untested. Not long afterwards, they escaped to Austria where meals were provided by the Red Cross who ran the refugee camp.

But there must have been a 'cooking gene' in my mother's DNA and once she got going, she was a natural. Hungarian cuisine is delicious and diverse – ranging from the richness of luscious stews and casseroles redolent with sour cream and herbs to roasts and fried meats. Soups are a particular speciality such as *Halászlé* – fish soup made with plump *pontye* – a trout-like freshwater fish – sautéed with onions, garlic and paprika. Chicken soup – a clear fragrant broth that takes eight hours to cook and is served with home-made noodles, chopped liver and tiny cubes of chicken breast. These dishes are all part of the High Cuisine of Hungary enjoyed by the aristocracy, upper and middle classes, accompanied by fine wines and even finer desserts. But what really sets Hungarian cooking apart is the variety of vegetarian recipes – created not through any form of political or ecological correctness but simply due to lack of meat.

In 1914, 75% of Hungarians lived on the land either as peasants indentured to rich landowners, living and working on huge estates, or as small-holders working their own tiny farms. For these people meat was something you ate once or twice each year – at Christmas and Easter if you were lucky. So, they developed a vast, delicious range of vegetarian meals – called *főzelék* – literally translated – 'cooked stuff'. Despite this unappetising translation, it is delicious. An enormous variety of meatless stews, all based on a roux made of flour browned in rendered pork fat, then thickened with water, stock or milk. Into this base went all sorts of vegetables such as green beans (*bab főzelék*) and cabbage (*caposta főzelék*). Just before serving, sour cream was stirred through and it was served with bread to mop up the sauce. On most days this was the entire meal. On a good – a very good – day, meat, pancetta or sausage was added.

In addition to *főzelék*, there also existed a variety of potato-based dishes such as *rakot krumpli* and *galushka*, as well as literally dozens of soups. All delicious and cheap to cook.

Frying the ingredients in rendered port fat gave these simple dishes their wonderful flavour. The bad news is that it also contributed to one of the highest rates of heart disease in Europe. Rich people cooked their food in rendered chicken, duck or even goose fat thereby creating an even more flavoursome though no less deadly meal.

When my mother first embarked on her culinary career, she had to rely on these 'peasant' recipes out of pure economic necessity. When she was a little girl, although she had watched her mother prepare these meals for the labourers on their estate, she had no idea how to do it herself. But she made it up as she went along and somehow managed to turn out plentiful, inexpensive, delicious meals. Ironically her main challenge was the same as she had faced in Hungary in her early married life – getting her hands on the right ingredients.

In 1957, Australia boasted an eye-popping abundance of fresh fruit and vegetables, meat and poultry. To newly arrived immigrants like my parents, the selection was staggering. This truly was a land of milk and honey. But much as my mother enjoyed milk and honey, what she actually needed for her cooking was garlic, parsley and paprika as well as pork fat. These were not available in any supermarket or the ubiquitous corner store that in those days was found on – um – every corner. Eventually she tracked down an Italian greengrocer in the next suburb. This took care of the vegies. Pork fat proved more challenging until a few months after they moved to Annandale, an enterprising young Hungarian butcher proceeded to not only supply all his compatriots in Sydney but the Poles, Czechs and Italians as well. He went on to make a well-deserved fortune and became a powerful business leader but to his early customers, he would be known forever by the affectionate nickname –'Salami Sam'.

My parents' home soon became the focal point of the local Hungarian community. Every weekend was party-time. The parties did not start until midnight as there was still much work to be done on the house, but most people turned up well before the appointed hour to lend a hand. And everyone brought something – by way of food or building materials. In 1958, if you were walking down a street in Annandale and passed a group of bright young people carrying a large bunch of carrots, a sack of potatoes, a bottle of cheap red wine and some 2 x 4 planks of timber, the chances are they were on their way to a knees-up at the Langs.

Once the major work was completed, it was time for my parents to leave the tradesmen (aka lodgers) to it and head off to buy furniture. When they first moved in, my parents possessed a double bed, a small kitchen table and two wooden chairs. Although each lodger was required to furnish their own room and provide a chair, the huge house still echoed like an aircraft hangar. It needed furniture. Lots of furniture.

Finances had improved marginally by this time and their bank account surged from absolutely zero to boasting the princely sum of 30 pounds. They were lucky – in the late fifties, anyone who could afford to redecorate was buying sleek modern furniture – wooden framed armchairs and sofas, spindly tables and teak pieces at prices my parents could not have dreamt of paying. But as it turned out, they could afford the cast-offs – huge sofas with rounded arms and soft padding, squishy armchairs big enough for two people, heavy ornate dining settings. Week after week these pieces were passed in at auction so when my parents turned up offering cash – even small amounts – they were met with open arms. Or even better – with free delivery.

Their 30-pound fortune turned out to be more than sufficient to furnish the entire house. Cavernous wardrobes, bedheads, dressing tables, a walnut dining suite comprising eight chairs, a table and a china cabinet, all intricately carved. A lounge suite – two sofas and two armchairs covered in a charmingly faded floral print. They even had enough left over for a box of crockery, a tray of cutlery and some bed and table linen. Although both my parents had come from middle-class families and prior to the Second World War (and the Soviet invasion) had lived surrounded by antique furniture, paintings and beautiful rugs, they were now over the moon at acquiring other people's castoffs. They had given up everything, risked their very lives to build a new life in Australia and here they were, owning a furnished house, which (and this was the best bit) they were most unlikely to lose to some marauding Russian!

I have a photograph of my parents in their newly furnished bedroom. Due to the absence of plaster dust I assume it was taken at least a year after they moved in. They smile into the camera – my mother in a white blouse and dark skirt, my father jacketless but wearing a tie. They look ridiculously young, relaxed, utterly content.

One evening some thirty years later, my husband and I were regaling my parents about our own renovation nightmare - wrong tiles delivered and laid, electrician gone AWOL, blah, blah. My parents began to reminisce about their first house. The backbreaking work for months on end, the broken windows, holey floors, cold showers all winter. The freezing rooms and general mayhem together with lack of money to do things properly and the many corners they had to cut. They made it seem very amusing, but I realised just how difficult it must have been. Feeling ashamed about my own complaints, I sympathised. "It sounds awful!"

But my mother laughed and shook her head. "Oh no – it was wonderful. We were so happy!"

Helen and Otto at the 'Dead House'

Helen and Otto – in their bedroom

The proud home-owners. And the best bit – this time, no marauding Russian was going to take it away from them!

CHAPTER 3
The Bullet List

It is fashionable these days to compile a Bucket List – a compendium of 'things I really must get around to doing before I die, otherwise I'll be seriously ticked off when I take my last breath!' I don't have one of these lists. To paraphrase John Lennon, I guess I'm too busy making other plans while life happens to me."

But I do have a Bullet List. A carefully considered register of people I'd gladly – ok, maybe not so gladly and I might not actually be smiling on impact – take a bullet for. It's a fairly short list and comprises members of my immediate family as well as a few other people.

The 'others' include my Year 12 English master. He was that rare and precious being – a born teacher, able to pass on his passion for literature to a gaggle of feckless 17-year old girls. His classes were pure delight as he taught me to appreciate the beauty of the English language, launching me on my life-long love affair with Shakespeare, Keats, Wordsworth, Yeats, Hopkins and other friends. All these years later, his parting words continue to hold true, "No situation in life is so difficult or tragic it can't be made more bearable by reading poetry."

Sadly, not all my teachers were as spot on with their advice. My Year 9 maths teacher promised that one day I would find a practical use for algebra and trigonometry. Sorry Miss S– I'm still waiting!

My friend Deb is on my Bullet List and not just because she knows where the bodies are buried. We met during our first year at university back when – as my daughter would say – dinosaurs walked the earth. Well not quite, but it was many years ago in what now feels like a much simpler, less frantic time. Although we didn't think so as we raced to lectures, juggled boyfriends and dreamed of one day – if not quite ruling the world – then at least being on first name terms with those who did.

During our first year, Deb and I lived in college until the vexations of bad food, hard beds and six showers between 14 students drove us to 'go flatting' by moving into a house near the university. Five of us embarked on this terribly grown-up adventure and despite the inevitable tensions (especially on Saturday nights) of now sharing two bathrooms between five girls, we had a wonderful time. We spent the entire summer holidays making the house habitable because it really wasn't when we signed the lease. It had been a university rental for years and had it been up for sale, would have earned the moniker, 'Renovators delight!' But we were young, had boundless energy and an army of boys we could call on to do the heavy lifting. Within three months, the house shone. So much so that when the Hong Kong based owner took it into his head to inspect it, he was so impressed he reduced our rent.

It was not your typical student dive. We had a cleaning roster, a cooking roster and most nights sat down to eat dinner together around our polished dining room table. While the food varied in quality depending on who was on duty, we were never short of chocolate Tim Tams and coffee. I won't hazard a guess at how much caffeine we consumed during those three years, but I suspect a small developing country out there owes us a debt of gratitude. And we were never short of visitors. Mostly of the male variety and understandably so. Five giggling girls, decent food, clean carpets, coffee. What's not to love?

Deb and I became close friends during this period in our lives. She was studying architecture while I was a law student and we found each other's world fascinating, although I suspect I drew the better deal. Deb had to hear – in mind-numbing detail – about each recent High Court decision while I got to help her build architectural models. This was great fun, although not without its dangers. Very late one night, we drove down to Coogee Beach and borrowed a bucket of sand. We almost got caught by the ranger, but it was worth the risk. Deb's stunning model of the Bell Tower in Lake Burley Griffin earned her High Distinction – due in no small part to the very realistic rendered 'sandstone' walls.

We stayed friends after university and finally in 2006, fulfilled our long-held dream of travelling around Europe together. Although I had been many times before, this trip was very special. Deb explained how gothic churches were constructed to represent the Trinity; the method by which Titian tinted his yellow paints to reflect light and myriad other fascinating things. She also tried to teach me how to read a map. It is proof of her nobility of character and great kindness that having seen me at my bumbling worst, she did not abandon me in the backstreets of Paris. We still meet at least once each month for dinner and after the first glass of champagne, giggle like teenagers long into the night.

My Kiwi buddy Justine is also on my Bullet List. It's not so much that she knows where the bodies are buried – its more accurate to say that due to her gentle wisdom and compassion over many years, I have kept the body count considerably lower than may otherwise have been the case. We have been friends now for over 25 years since, as the expression goes, "She had me at hello." Or more accurately at *Zdravstvuite*.

We met in Russian language class, initially thrown together because we were the only Mature Age Students (i.e. over 20 years old) and of non-Russian background. The nearest either of us came to having a Russian ancestor was the officer who commandeered my father's childhood home back in 1948. Unlike the rest of our class, who capitalised on their bilingual heritage and surfeit of Russian grandparents by enrolling in a subject where an A-plus grade was a shoe-in.

But for Justine and me, it was sheer hard slog. We struggled with the Cyrillic alphabet, insanely complex grammar, elusive verbs and Humiliation 101 every Monday morning when we had to read out our 'What I Did This Weekend' compositions. My riveting tales of, "Got up very early, did the grocery shopping, washed the dog, cooked, cleaned out the pantry, ironed, gardened, cleaned the house and drove my stepchildren all around Sydney," drew amused smiles from our classmates. And the suggestion from our Russian teacher that I needed to inject some breaks into the sentence. As my weekend had not actually contained any 'breaks', I found this advice singularly unhelpful. But the most challenging part of this exercise was using the correct verb for 'driving'. Not a simple task as Russian is blessed with a surfeit of verbs for this activity but only one that correctly implies you took the kids somewhere and then brought them back home again. And I always did. Often in the face of great temptation.

Meanwhile Larissa, Vladimir, Olga, Vera, Dmitry, Anna and their comrades described parties, sleeping, lounging around and going out for coffee in such sophisticated language that Justine and I swung giddily between consuming jealousy of their undemanding lives and admiration of their facility with Russian nouns, adjectives and adverbs.

The seal on our friendship was a five-week intensive language course we attended together in St Petersburg. In fact, being together was the only way we survived. We took turns lugging eight litre containers of water up 13 flights of stairs. (In July, many apartment buildings in Russia have the water supply switched off for maintenance – who knew?) By the time we came home, we had biceps to die for, slightly more Russian grammar at our disposal and a life-long friendship.

So, as you can see, to score a place on my Bullet List if you are not actually a blood relative, you need to do something pretty amazing and terrific. Over a sustained period. Against all odds.

Or you have to save a life. Literally.

This is why a few weeks after the terrible Chocolate Gourmet Cookies Disaster of 2010, I added another name to my Bullet List. Dr N is one of Australia's most brilliant lung cancer specialists but more than this, he is a gentle, unassuming man of great integrity. A true gentleman who gave my family hope when we had pretty much run out of that commodity, as well as an even more precious gift. He gave us time. Eight wonderful, glorious months.

When we first went to see him, my mother was fading fast. This is not intended to be a dramatic turn of phrase; she really was shrinking before our eyes. Every day she grew thinner and smaller and I watched the light within her fade. My mother had always been such a vibrant, energetic woman who bustled and sped through life with passion and zest. It was gut-wrenching to witness her demise.

For six months after being diagnosed with lung cancer, my mother did the rounds of doctors and clinics, was subjected to extensive chemotherapy and a variety of tests and procedure. She bore it all bravely. But the hardest part of the whole horrible experience was the inevitable question, "Were you a heavy smoker?" And the implied criticism this carried.

It was so unfair. My mother had never, ever smoked and neither had my father. Cigarette smoke was strictly verboten in their home. It was the only thing that rendered my mother anything less than over-the-top hospitable. Any guest at my parents' home who even looked like they were thinking about lighting up was requested – politely but firmly – to do so between courses. Outside. In the smoke-haze of the 60s and 70s, this turned every gathering into a progressive dinner with guests moving seamlessly between the dining room and the back garden. Even in the middle of winter there were no exceptions to the rule. I once commented that the forlorn group of men standing under the gum tree on a June evening looked very cold.

"Good!" my mother responded.

But as soon as the offending cigarette was finished, and the shamefaced guest came back inside, she plied him with food and drink, spoiling and cossetting him once more. Rather like a mother to the wayward child who does something very naughty but then repents and is forgiven. Heavy smokers who made more than one trip outside merited the same sad shake of the head that mother would give to the child who reoffended.

When I grew old enough to want to try my hand at some adult vices of my own, smoking didn't even enter the equation. Instinctively I knew that if I was to remain on good terms with my mother, I had to pick other foibles. And lying about it was not an option either – she had a nose like a bloodhound. The same overdeveloped olfactory sense that enabled her to select a ripe melon at five metres put paid to that.

When my mother was diagnosed with lung cancer, my initial response was, "Are you sure?" Unfortunately, they were. Being a fully paid up, if not founding, member of the Australia Anti-smoking League clearly afforded no guarantee against this horrible disease. Approximately 20% of all sufferers never smoked – their cancer is the result of a random genetic mutation. Pure bloody bad luck, as a sympathetic nurse explained to me.

Yes, bloody, bloody bad luck. And also, deeply humiliating for my mother because most people initially assumed that her illness was divine retribution for her three packs a day habit. As the disease took its toll, she no longer had the energy to disabuse them. So, by the time we went to see the lung guru, we were at a very low point. The cancer was winning and much as I tried to pretend that everything was fine, it was not.

But Dr N changed all this. From the first moment I saw him – a slim, dapper man, immaculately dressed in a beautifully cut dark blue suit, white shirt and stripped tie, I felt hope – that long absent friend – stir in my heart. He ushered us into his surgery and shut the door. Unlike the other doctors, Dr N didn't sit behind a big desk to separate himself from his patient. He sat down right next to my mother and said, "I'm sorry this is happening. It must be really difficult for you." And he meant it.

My mother nodded.

"I see from the notes that you weren't a smoker, so this cancer is one of those inexplicable ones. They just happen. It's very unfair."

My mother nodded again. He reached over and took her hand.

I wanted to kiss him. I wanted to whoop Apache style and gallop around his surgery. Here finally – thank You, Lord! – was someone who understood. Even if he couldn't offer her anything else, he was giving her respect and compassion.

And then he proceeded to give her the gift of time. When we left his surgery an hour later, clutched in my sweaty palm was a prescription for a new drug. Just starting clinical trials and although originally designed for liver cancer, it was now being considered as a potential treatment for lung cancer. Not yet commonly prescribed for this but my mother's tumour had already metastasized into her liver so she qualified for the trial.

Going down in the lift, my mother hugged me. Dr N had carefully and painstakingly explained that there was only a one in five chance that this medication would have any effect and even if it did, it was only a 'treatment'. It was not a cure, and no-one could predict how long it would continue to work. We listened attentively. We nodded at appropriate intervals. We tried to look intelligent and promised ourselves that later on, we would be realistic. But right now, we allowed ourselves the luxury of raging optimism.

Making it seem even more like witchcraft, Dr N also explained that for the lucky percentage of people the drug helps, the first sign is a skin rash. And not just any rash – the tsunami of rashes. The rashi-est rash of all. Covering the entire body. Not itchy, fades rapidly although looks pretty awful while it lasts. But if this does occur, it's a clear indication that the treatment has kicked in and the patient will start to feel better almost immediately. It all sounded seriously weird, but we were not in any position to argue. We could only wait.

Wait we did – for the next twenty days. I grew more frustrated and panicky as nothing happened. My mother grew weaker. Soon after she was diagnosed, she made me promise not to visit her every day, but we were in daily phone contact. Every morning now before I called, I spent a few minutes psyching myself to sound positive and up-beat irrespective of her response, trying to pitch my, "And how are you today?" at just the right level of nonchalance mixed with mild interest. No big deal. Just wondering how you are feeling? No reason really. Not important. Except it was.

And every morning, her voice ever fainter, my mother replied, "Not good."

Before adding sadly, "I'm sorry." The apology usually undid me, and I rushed to get off the phone before I – to quote my daughter – "Lost it. Like, totally." I was so angry. How dare she be sorry! How dare she act as if this was her fault! It wasn't anyone's fault – which was a damn shame because I really wanted to kill someone. Maybe then I could stay sane a bit longer. One morning, I misplaced my self-control to such a degree that I kicked my study wall. Really hard. So hard it made a big dent. I spent the rest of the day hobbling around while trying to work out how to tell my husband what I had done without causing him to use the words 'slightly' and 'unhinged' in the same sentence.

Then, just as I was running out of pretending and my mother was running out of time, it happened. Exactly three weeks after our meeting with Dr N, my mother called me at 5.30 in the morning. I was still asleep and consequently not firing on all cylinders when I grabbed the phone.

"I'm covered in a rash. All over. Even inside my mouth."

A rash. Dear God, what else could go wrong?

A rash! Dear God! I yelled loudly enough to wake the rest of my family and rushed around getting dressed.

A rash! Yes!

I raced over. Because of the crazy hour, there was little traffic and even better – no police and I did it in record time without getting arrested. As I screeched to a halt outside her house, I saw for the first time in many months, the front door was wide open. The smell of fresh coffee wafted towards me. I ran inside. My mother stood at her usual place by the sink, putting mugs onto a tray. She was emaciated and painfully thin, swamped by her now too big orange apron. Her entire face and neck was covered by a bright red rash. But she was smiling, her eyes bright and alive. We had been granted our miracle.

And it truly was a miracle! Her appetite improved the same day. Over the next week, she stopped losing weight, then quickly began to regain the weight she had lost. Most importantly, her energy returned, and she felt well again.

But we both knew she was living on borrowed time. I knew it and I knew she knew it too as I watched her throw herself back into the life she had put on hold. She began to plan another trip to Hungary in June, "To see everyone one more time." She caught up with old friends and gave dinner parties. She spent as much time as possibly with her two adored granddaughters and – for me best of all – she ensured that the catastrophe of the shop bought biscuits would never, ever be repeated. She taught me to bake.

In my defence, I need to put on record that I was not a total klutz in the kitchen. In fact, I could – and regularly did – turn out tasty meals. Also, I was a dab hand at giving formal dinner parties. The food – or so the feedback went – was delicious and innovative, although this was due more to the expensive ingredients I used than any innate skill. But I had no idea how to prepare traditional Hungarian cuisine – simple, tasty dishes often pulled together using basic, cheap bits and pieces that you just happen to have in the pantry. And – as had become blindingly obvious to my mother's friends – I. Could. Not. Bake.

Strawberry mousse – yes. Tiramisu – yes. Rhubarb crumble – yes. But four-layer chocolate cake, linzer tort, black forest cherry cake? No. No. And no.

When I turned up for coffee one morning and found my mother elbows deep in recipe books about to start a mega baking session, her suggestion that I 'might like to watch and maybe learn something?' was less than enthusiastically received. But I stayed and watched her effortlessly work her magic. By the end of that session, I was hooked.

It became our regular Tuesday morning ritual. Initially I was just the fascinated observer but soon I began to beat and cream and mix as the daunting task of baking became less so. We must have baked on rainy days, on cold days, on overcast days but in my memory, it is always summer. The bright cheerful kitchen, sunlight dancing on the ocean and the hum of the waves beyond the patio doors. The aroma of chocolate, vanilla, cinnamon rising from the oven, mingling with the scent of fresh coffee while we mixed and measured, laughed and talked.

Each recipe had a history; some funny, some poignant. On those mornings, a long line of people trooped through the kitchen. Long dead but not forgotten – my mother shared their recipes and recounted their stories. The village postmaster's wife – a woman rendered silent and taciturn by the tragic loss of her husband and only child just before World War II. She had no friends and ran the post office with monosyllabic efficiency but for some reason, she took a shine to my mother. Every Sunday after church, she walked the little girl to her own home, sat her on a high stool and plied her with delicious apple cake, while she combed and plaited my mother's beautiful curly hair. Although the apple cake recipe was a closely guarded family secret, on my mother's wedding day, the woman gave her the recipe together with a little silver comb.

The ancient nun at my mother's school who – to the amusement of the students – spent most of the day asleep by the fire in the dining room. But once a week, she came into her own while she taught the girls how to prepare sophisticated desserts. Her profiteroles were works of art as her arthritic hands twirled and twisted the melted sugar in the saucepan to create spun toffee as fine as spider webs. Then, wimple askew, in a final triumphant sweeping gesture, she poured this onto the cream-filled puffs to create a visual and a culinary masterpiece. To her everlasting regret, my mother never quite perfected this technique.

One day, I faced my nemesis – chocolate hazelnut biscuits. My mother deciphered the code. "Not ready… beat it some more…"

Showing me how to aerate the mixture, then stop and gently roll a small amount in my fingers. It disintegrated, so she told me to beat it some more – just a little bit more. This time, when I rolled, the mixture obligingly formed a symmetrical moist ball.

"Perfect!" she pronounced. Feeling skilful and ridiculously proud of myself, I rolled it out, cut it into rounds and placed the tray into the oven. Fifteen minutes later, the fragrant little discs emerged. I let them cool, then sandwiched pairs together with cherry jam before carefully dipping them in melted chocolate.

I was hot and sweaty, splattered in melted chocolate, exhausted and totally exhilarated. As we sat down to drink coffee and eat the fruits of my labour, I asked, "Whose recipe is this?"

"This one is mine. I invented it years ago for your father. Do you remember how much he liked hazelnut and chocolate? Now – it's yours. And you must pass it on."

So, I am.

Recipe for chocolate hazelnut biscuits

Ingredients:

1/2 cup roasted hazelnuts (or 1/3 cup hazelnut meal/flour if you can get it)

½ cup butter. Preferably unsalted

½ cup caster sugar

½ cup plain flour. You can use wholemeal flour too. That make the biscuits chewier.

1/3 block Lindt dark chocolate – at least 60% cocoa

¼ teaspoon salt – but only if using unsalted butter.

Method:

- If using whole hazelnuts, preheat oven to 180 degrees. Fan forced – 160 degrees. Place in single layer onto baking sheet covered oven tray. Roast for around 12 minutes. But keep checking it doesn't burn. Hazelnuts should be light brown colour. Not dark brown.

- While still hot, rub hazelnuts in clean tea towel to remove skin.

- Cool in refrigerator then pulse hazelnuts in food processor until ground. DO NOT overgrind – you don't want to turn it into a paste.

- Reduce oven temperature to 160 degrees (140 degrees fan forced)

- Beat softened butter with sugar in an electric mixer until light and fluffy. It will change colour from yellow to pale cream. Should take around 3 minutes.

- Add sifted flour and ground hazelnuts (and salt if using). Beat on low speed until a soft dough forms.

- Mixture should be slightly sticky - but not too sticky. If it's too dry, add tepid water a teaspoon at a time until you get the right consistency. You can test this by taking a teaspoon of the mixture. Roll it into a ball with your hands. It should feel firm but not hard. Sticky but not too sticky. (This gets easier with practice – I promise!)

- Once it's the right consistency, roll dough into balls – about 1 inch in diameter. Place each ball onto a tray lined with baking paper, leaving plenty of space between each one. Use a fork to flatten each ball. Bake (160 degrees or 140 degrees fan forced) until golden. You may need to rotate the baking sheet half way through. Do not overcook – they can burn easily.

- Leave to cool slightly. Then transfer biscuits to a wire rack and cool completely.

- Meanwhile, melt chocolate in microwave – or double boiler – until completely melted.

- Gently dip each biscuit into the melted chocolate, making sure each side is coated. Place on plate lined in baking paper until chocolate has set.

- Biscuits can be stored in airtight container for up to a week.

CHAPTER 4
Echoes

British novelist L P Hartley declared, "The past is a foreign country: they do things differently there." For so many of us here in Australia, our past *is* a foreign country. Mine is Hungary.

Although I grew up here and love Australia, my frequent trips back to my ancestral homeland are highlights. Catching up with family and friends, eating enormous meals, spending time in Budapest – surely one of the world's loveliest cities. Gourmet food, wonderful wines, concerts, eating in the fabulous restaurants. Exquisite patisseries. Picnics in the country, swimming in Lake Balaton. And did I mention the food?

I come back to Australia relaxed, rejuvenated and considerably rounder. Usually about five kgs rounder and over the next gruelling months of salad, long walks and no alcohol, I vow and declare I'll never overeat in Hungary again. Of course, I always do.

It took me almost two years to summon up the courage to return to Hungary after my mother died. There was so much to do in Sydney – sell her house, sort through an entire lifetime of stuff… But the truth was I kept putting it off. While my everyday life helped me blot out the pain of losing her, I knew that amid those gently rolling Hungarian hills and loving relatives, there would be no escape from my grief. I knew it would be painful. I also suspected it would be immensely healing. It was.

I spent the first week back there surrounded by family and friends. We talked about my mother, we cried and laughed and celebrated her life – lived so generously and well across two continents. I talked to people who had known her long before she immigrated to Australia and began to get yet another perspective on her life as a child and young woman. As their reminiscences brought the past – her past – vividly to life for me, I yearned to experience for myself some of the places that had formed her.

So, on a beautiful autumn day I find myself standing in the town square in Pápa, a small town 60 km north of Budapest. Pronounced *Paapa* (long a) – its name means 'pope', testament to the 13 churches in the city. The Franciscan Friars (a Catholic teaching order) settled here in the middle ages, followed soon after by the Paulines. From this time onwards, Pápa played a significant role in the religious history of Europe. Exemplifying Hungary's religious tolerance at a time when not all countries were as enlightened. The first Hungarian translation of Martin Luther's Catechism of Heidelberg was printed in Pápa in 1577 and the town became a major centre of Eastern European Protestantism during the late Middle Ages.

As my long-suffering husband and daughter will attest, history is my passion – although the word 'obsession' has on occasion and rather unkindly (in my opinion), been bandied about. Our family holidays to Europe include stimulating educational excursions to obscure places while I track down yet another derelict monument, shrine or building where someone vaguely famous once spent a night. Or thought of spending the night. Or never even considered spending the night but merely rode past. Around 50% of the time, we actually locate these places. And even when we don't – well, let me assure you, travel guides merely skim the surface of sightseeing.

But today I am on a much more personal quest. In the distant days of the 1940s, my mother was a boarder at one of the many convent schools that flourished in this town until the Soviet occupation.

This is not my first visit to Pápa. I came here years ago for Midnight Mass during my first visit back to Hungary. My mother, brother and I were spending Christmas with my mother's family in a village about 15km away and I persuaded my uncle to drive me here to church. No-one else was prepared to risk the numbing cold and slippery roads or possibly was so overfed they couldn't actually stand up.

I felt very virtuous as we set off in the darkness, unaware that my uncle's willingness to take me stemmed from his desire to smoke quietly in the car for an hour or two away from his older sister's murderous glare.

I don't remember anything about the town or much about the service. But I do recall the welcoming warmth of the vast cathedral packed with hundreds of worshippers, the evocative scent of incense, polished wood and centuries of dust, the angelic sound of the choir. And I will never forget that as I spilled out with the crowd to wait on the square for my uncle's car, it began to snow. I watched snowflakes swirl gently down in a spiral, each one a different pattern, intricate and delicate beyond describing. Long accustomed to this miracle, everyone else hurried away home while I stood transfixed, my arm outstretched to catch the gleaming flakes on my blue velvet sleeve. At that moment, church bells rang out above my head to proclaim the birth of the Christ Child. It is one of the most beautiful things I ever experienced and the loveliest Christmas gift I ever received.

So much has changed in Hungary since that long-ago Christmas. Once only tolerated within very strict limits by the authoritarian state, religion is again flourishing. Towns like Pápa, with their baroque churches and soaring cathedral, are prospering from the tourist trade. Standing at the edge of the square, I admire the recent extensive renovations. Everything is clean and bright – from the pale granite slabs on the square to the planter boxes filled with colourful blooms and the numerous cafés with their stripped awnings and white wicker chairs and tables. Even the fountain in the centre has been restored. The slender bronze girl once again proudly lifts her hands, balancing the pitcher on her head while cascades of water play around her feet.

Although I came to Pápa to visit the convent where my mother spent so many happy years and it is only a short walk away, I decide to first fortify myself with coffee. The coffee is hot and strong. As I drink it, I try to remember what my mother told me about her time here. Sadly, I realise I really don't know much at all about those four years. But I do know how it ended – tragically and unexpectedly. The convent had survived the horror of the war years, but it could not withstand the brutality of the Soviet occupation.

Embittered by the loss of territory after the First World War through the infamous Treaty of Trianon, in the 1930's many Hungarians favoured closer economic ties with Hitler's newly emerging Germany and its seductive promises of restoration. A fatal mistake but by the time most people realised, it was too late. When war broke out in September 1939, Hungary was determined to remain neutral but for a country as geographically strategic as it is, this was never going to be a realistic option. In 1940, under increasing economic and military pressure from Germany, Hungary joined the Axis Powers. Though even now – naively – it hoped to avoid direct involvement in the war. But then in 1941, Herr Hitler forced the government's hand and soon Hungarian forces were participating in the invasion of Yugoslavia and in Operation Barbarossa – the invasion of the Soviet Union.

Hungary soon realised (tragically true to form) it had again chosen the wrong side and tried to extricate herself. While continuing to fight alongside Germany, the Hungarian Regent, Admiral Horthy, began secret negotiations with the United States and England for a separate peace. Hitler discovered this in March 1944, immediately dispatching German forces into Hungary to occupy the recalcitrant country and force it back into the fold. With the majority of Hungarians now desperate to break free from Germany and avoid the carnage that would inevitably result from the anticipated attack by the Soviet Union, Horthy signed a not-so-secret armistice with the USSR.

Two weeks later, in a plot twist worthy of a John le Carré novel, Horthy's son was kidnapped by the German SS and spirited back to German, rolled in a carpet. Desperate to save him, Horthy revoked the armistice. But it was too late. The Nazis deposed Horthy and replaced him with Hungarian fascist leader, Ferenc Szálasi. With German backing, Szálasi established a new government. Hungary's fate was sealed. She would pay a very heavy price for being on the losing side yet again.

The tide of war turned against the Nazis and their reluctant Hungarian allies. The Russian army surged into Hungary in February 1944 and the desperate, bloody battle for Budapest claimed tens of thousands of lives. By the following spring, Russian troops occupied the entire country. Approximately 400,000 Hungarian soldiers and over 600,000 civilians died in the Second World War. Although the war in Europe ended in May 1945, the USSR had no intention of letting go of this hard-won prize. The cessation of hostilities did not mean a return to peace in Hungary.

Amid great fanfare in November 1945, Hungary held 'free democratic elections'. Except they were anything but free. Russian soldiers were everywhere in evidence manning polling booths and intimidating voters. Nor were the elections in any way democratic – convoys of soldiers ferried communist supporters around the country to exercise their voting rights again and again. But despite these bully-boy tactics, most of the voters refused to be intimidated and the Hungarian Communist Party only polled 17% of the original vote. The people had spoken.

But the communists had their own agenda and had no intention of listening. The occupying Russian forces invited the Hungarian Communist Party to form a government, ostensibly to 'ensure the peaceful existence' of the country. Or so went the story they spun to the rest of the world.

Under Moscow's watchful eye, the new government began a sweeping round of socialist 'reforms'. The Hungarian monarchy was formally abolished in February 1946 and replaced by the Republic of Hungary. In August 1949, the degradation of this fiercely proud and independent country into a satellite of the Soviet Union was complete with the establishment of the People's Republic of Hungary.

The Catholic Church had been a thorn in the side of the communist regime from the very beginning. Clearly it needed a firm hand. In 1946, the State confiscated all church property and two years later, an edict was passed closing all religious orders. What followed was quick and brutal.

Since the late eighteenth century, the Sisters of the Carmelite Order had lived out their vocation to God by teaching and caring for girls and their school in Pápa was justly famous throughout the country. Many of the Sisters were highly intelligent, well-educated women who had been watching political developments anxiously. Beneath their serene countenances and downcast eyes, they must have realised the danger they faced right on their doorstep. Since 1944, Pápa had been occupied by Russian soldiers, many of them billeted in the Esterhazy Palace around the corner from the convent. They also took over the cathedral and in a matter of days stripped it bare. Seeming to delight in causing as much damage as possible, the soldiers smashed the ancient stained-glass windows, stabled their horses in the exquisite little Lady Chapel and used the main altar as a latrine.

Once the war ended, everyone hoped and prayed the soldiers would go home but instead, their numbers swelled. The residents of Pápa lived quietly, trying to ignore the Russians in their midst, hoping to 'live and let live'. Initially, in spite of many wanton acts of destruction of property, the troops remained fairly well behaved. But they were only biding their time until 1948 when the new government delivered absolute power into their hands.

Shortly after the elections, the Reverend Mother of the convent had a visitation from the local Russian commander. Unlike most of his ilk, he was polite and respectful. He informed her that in two days' time, the convent would be 'nationalised'. Anyone found still on the premises would be arrested.

The Reverend Mother thanked him for letting her know and politely showed him out. Ignoring the anxious faces of the Sisters, she went back into her room. She had been expecting something like this for months and was as serene as ever when she emerged a short time later to pass on the news to the others. No-one panicked – there was too much to do. Whatever fate awaited them, they needed to make sure the girls in their charge were not caught up in it. The students must all go home. School was breaking up early this year.

Helping the girls pack their belongings ready to leave, some of the younger Sisters became flustered at the unaccustomed break in their routine. The girls were excited and soon the normally peaceful corridors buzzed with noise. The older Sisters and Mother Superior remained calm and focused while they contacted the parents.

Trunks packed and waiting in the coach-house, that evening the school assembled for the last time to celebrate Sunday Mass as best it could. The doors of the cathedral had been nailed shut and soldiers stood guard around the square. The three priests had already been taken away and so there was no-one to conduct Mass or give Communion. The Mother Superior led the girls in the service and at the appropriate time, dispensed the unsanctified host to her little congregation. "Our Lord understands that we have to do it this way," she assured them. Mass in Hungarian churches always ended with the singing of the national anthem and the evocative words and haunting melody echoed around the room. Soon it would be an offense punishable by death to sing or even whistle the anthem and although they didn't know it then, didn't yet comprehend the horrors to come, some girls wept. A little frightened now, a little sad to be going home so unexpectedly. Long after their charges were in bed, the Sisters continued kneeling in prayer. Whatever was about to descend upon them was in God's hands and their faith remained unshaken.

Anxious parents arrived the next day to take their daughters home. Petrol was an impossible luxury now even for those lucky few who had managed to hang on to their cars and the forlorn little groups made their way on foot to the train station half a kilometre away. They had to walk past Russian soldiers sitting along the fence of the Esterhazy Castle. The soldiers chewed sunflower seeds as they watch them go by. They spat the husks at the passing parade. Whenever anyone scored a direct hit, their comrades laughed and cheered loudly.

Back at home, my mother found that the novelty and unaccustomed freedom soon wore thin. She missed her friends. She missed the routine and she missed some of the Sisters. Her mother assured her that it would only be for a little while – just until things return to normal. In the meantime, my mother embroidered a handkerchief for her favourite Sister. A few days before the Sister's birthday, she wrapped it carefully and together with a note, committed it to the vagrancies of the postal system. The parcel came back to her two months later. It had been sliced open. The note and gift were missing. "Not known at this address" was scrawled across the front in big red letters.

In the days that followed the evacuation of the school, many of the Sisters returned to their homes but some, including the Reverend Mother, disappeared forever without trace within the brutal prison regime. As for the convent itself, throughout the 1950s and 60 it served as the barracks for the ever-growing Russian army before being left trashed and abandoned. One of the town's primary schools was relocated here in the 1980s and in the early 90's it was turned into a high school. Whenever my mother was in Hungary over the years she always caught up with her few surviving school-friends and even attended a 40th anniversary reunion. But she never came back here although I recall her telling me only a few years ago that she had heard the building and grounds were being extensively restored.

So, fortified with coffee and memories, I am standing in front of the heavy oak door. I don't know what I will find beyond the thick sandstone walls. A remnant of the peace and serenity of the Carmelite Sisters? A reminder of the mindless brutality of the Soviet regime? Or a modern high school apparently very highly regarded in Hungarian educational circles? I know it is impossible but what I so desperately want to find is an echo of my mother. Of the wide-eyed little country girl who lived here through the war years and left here amid the turmoil that came after. I long for a tiny echo, no matter how faint.

Taking a deep breath, I bang the brass knocker and wait. Nothing happens. I try again. Still nothing. Then I notice an intercom by the door, looking totally out of place in the ornately carved wall. I press it. A few seconds later, I'm standing in the huge dark entry-hall, shaking hands with a friendly woman. One of the administrative staff, she has agreed to show me around.

The convent is an impressive building or more accurately, four buildings joined by archways set around a courtyard. My guide proudly points out the elaborate staircase and the beautiful stained-glass windows gleaming on three sides of it. When I ask if the windows and staircase are original, she tells me, sadly they are not. This part of the convent was completely rebuilt in the 1990's – restoration was impossible due to the extent of the damage.

She takes me into the courtyard, a cool and peaceful haven. She confirms that this was also totally rebuilt only eight years ago. We go upstairs. I know this is where the dormitories and nuns' cells used to be but there is no trace of them now as I am shown through modern well-equipped classrooms that stand waiting for the start of the new school year. With a proud flourish, my guide shows me the state-of-the art Language Lab and I make appropriately complementary noises. No doubt this is a very impressive educational institution – a wonderful place to teach and to learn. But it is modern, pristine, completely devoid of the past. I am so disappointed I could cry.

Carefully hiding my distress, I accompany her back downstairs. I thank her and prepare to leave. Then I look up. My eyes have become accustomed to the darkness and I can now see the faintest outlines of frescoes on the soaring ceiling. She obligingly flicks a light-switch and suddenly the scene is illuminated by the enormous brass chandelier. Pale blue sky, cream clouds, faded angels. Hands folded in prayer, their wings spread out in benediction, angels soar over my head while my guide explains that this historical relic survived only because it had been concealed beneath a false ceiling.

I close my eyes and listen. The past returns. I can hear the quiet swish of the Sisters' long habits. The faint click of the rosary beads at their waists when they walk by. And on the floor above, furtive whispers and giggles as the girls move around. This is what I came here for – the past come alive again – if only in my imagination.

There is more. As an afterthought, my guide offers to take me into the basement, which houses the original kitchen of the convent. We go down the steep stone stairs. Each step is shiny with age, slightly indented in the centre. Worn away over the years by thousands of footsteps, including my mother's.

In spite of the warm day, the kitchen is cold and dim, its three windows boarded up. Obviously, money for renovations didn't extend to this part of the building but at least the ceiling light still works. In the corner stands an enormous enamelled stove, partly obscured by wooden crates. Now it is easy to conjure up the past – the delighted girls watching the ancient nun with her wimple flying as she creates elaborate cakes. I tell the guide the story of the profiteroles. She smiles politely. It means nothing to her. It all happened long, long before she was born. In another time. Another country.

Back on the street, I'm blinking in the bright sunlight after we say goodbye. But before she goes inside, she points to a small brass plaque at the side of the door. I hadn't noticed it before but now I read, 'Here stood the Carmelite convent from 1794 until it was closed by the Soviets in 1948. This plaque is in loving and respectful memory of past teachers and students.' It was worth making the long journey just for this.

I walk slowly back to the square. I hadn't realised how emotionally exhausting revisiting the past would be. I'm not hungry. Just hollow and in dire need of comfort. I need cake. Lots of cake. I never eat cake back home but here in Hungary, I seem to be consuming it on a daily basis. Sometimes more than once a day. Luckily my train doesn't leave for over an hour, so I have time to indulge.

The cafés around the square are full of tourists enjoying the sunshine. But I don't feel like company, don't want the present to intrude quite yet. I turn away from the noisy groups and go along one of the little lanes that run down the hill. It is so narrow that three people walking abreast would find it cosy, but this has not stopped a couple of the residents from parking their cars along it. I clamber clumsily around one car and squeeze myself between two others. This is not fun, and I've almost decided to abandon the obstacle course and go back to join the tourists when I see a doorway marked *Pékség*. I don't so much see it as fall into it while negotiating my way around another bumper-bar. Impressed by an establishment with the confidence to simply call itself a bakery, amid the cafés, patisseries and even a *Milke Barre* courting visitors along the tourist strip, I venture inside.

It really is a bakery, complete with two women wearing flour-covered overalls toiling in front of a huge oven. I can smell coffee. Above the long counter hangs a blackboard announces *kávé*

– *300 forint. Sütemény* – *400 forint.* The menu is as unpretentious as the establishment's name. For less than $2 you get coffee and if you are feeling extravagant, another $2 will buy you *sütemény*, – literally translated – 'a baked thing'.

Just what I need. Hoping they hadn't seen my inelegant entry, I smile brightly and walk over to the counter. The older woman completely ignores me as she gets on with taking something hot and fragrant out of the oven with an implement that looks like a wide oar. But the other woman gives me a beady look, wipes her hands slowly on her apron and comes over.

"*Igen?*" Technically this means 'yes' but it also – I'm hoping – indicates she wants to take my order. Just for a moment, I toy with requesting a skinny decaf soy latte and a raspberry friand. But sanity prevails. Summoning up my best Hungarian, I ask for coffee and a Baked Thing. She nods and walks into the back room before I can enquire whether there is a choice of 'Things' or is it just 'Thing of the Day'?

She reappears a few seconds later. Maybe she was impressed by my masterful command of the language or maybe she just wants me out of her workspace, but she tells me I can eat outside, pointing to a half open door on the other side of the room. Feeling like I've stumbled (literally) into the Eastern European version of Faulty Towers, I obey and find myself in a beautiful courtyard. It is tiny. And perfect – two little tables and four chairs set on a small patch of grass surrounded by massed red and pink geraniums in tall pots. Roses in full bloom cascades down the wall of the bakery, the heady evocative fragrance adding the final touch.

I sit at one of the tables. The woman appears with my order, puts it down in front of me and goes back inside. I sip the coffee – served in a *demi-tasse* cup and black as pitch. It is delicious, but my attention is focused on the Baked Thing. A slice of poppy-seed cake covered with a light dusting of icing sugar. Not a sign of the sweet whipped cream most patisseries in Europe insist on providing. The cake is still warm. Its scent rises to meet me. As I inset my fork, thick orange syrup flows out of the cake's centre. This looks very promising.

I taste it. It is sublime! Ambrosial! Not too sweet, richly textured with a hint of poppy-seed overlaid by orange syrup. It is without doubt one of the best cakes I've eaten in a long time. The combination of cake and coffee is wonderful, and I consume them slowly, reverently. All too soon, the plate is clean. Barely able to stop myself from licking it, I go inside and order the same again. No doubt I will regret the second coffee at around 2am, and the cake when I next try to pull on my jeans, but right now, I'm beyond caring.

The woman brings out my order. She even smiles as she puts it in front of me. Encouraged by this, I tell her how wonderful it tastes. She accepts the compliment graciously and goes back inside while I attack the cake. This time I do – well not actually lick the plate – but run my finger along it to savour the last drops of syrup. I sit happily for a few more minutes in the sunshine until it's time to go. Thank goodness the walk to the station is downhill. Uphill may not be possible in my current condition.

I pay the bill, adding a gratuity that brings it to the princely sum of $20. The woman tries to give me change but I insist it's a tip. Shaking her head at the crazy extravagant tourist, she watches me waddle out. But about to step across the threshold into the lane, I realise that there is no way I'll be able to negotiate the cars in my overfed state. Not without damaging them or getting wedged between them. The older woman, who has been watching me, beckons me back into the courtyard. She unlocks the gate and lets me out into a lane, which to my surprise and relief is both wide and car-free. Telling me it leads to the cathedral, she goes back inside to bake more delicious 'Things'.

I set out for the station to catch the train back to Győr. My aunt and cousin are expecting me for dinner. As always, it will be a substantial and delicious meal ending with – God have mercy! – more cake. Which, to my shame, I will probably eat.

Attempting to walk off the avalanche of calories, I take the longer route through the *Vár Kert*- the garden of the Esterházy Palace. In a few months the palace will be ready to receive visitors but at the moment, it is still shrouded in scaffolding, windows boarded up. It's not actually a palace – more a very large mansion. But in the Austro–Hungary of the Hapsburgs, the immensely wealthy Esterházy family was the closest thing Hungarians had to their own home-grown royalty, so they were allowed to exaggerate.

The Pápa estate is only one of their many homes scattered around Hungary and Austria. My favourite is Esterháza Palace in Fertod. Completed in 1760 and considered one of the most expensive constructions in Europe at the time, it was commissioned by Prince Nikolas Esterházy. From 1766 until 1790, the celebrated composer Joseph Haydn lived and worked there under Nikolas's patronage. Many of Haydn's symphonies were first performed in the private opera house attached to the palace. Since Esterháza was restored several years ago, annual concerts are held there. Once again, Haydn's haunting music fills the rooms.

Esterháza Palace is a baroque gem of 126 rooms and vast grounds, an architectural masterpiece to rival Vienna's Schonbrunn but I think its greatest claim to fame is the dead straight road running from the gate directly north 101 km to the Esterházy palace in Vienna and 180km south to their palace in Budapest. A favourite pastime of young Esterházy princes was to set out at midnight after a sumptuous dinner and race each other. Whooping and yelling all the way, stopping only to change horses, it was a spectacular exhibition of testosterone fuelled excess. Yes, I suspect alcohol was involved.

The Esterházys rarely used their home in Pápa and it was in pristine condition when the Russian army seized it for their headquarters in 1944. By the time they decamped a few years later, the estate was in ruins. The officers made themselves comfortable in the sumptuous first floor suites, the common soldiers were billeted in the stables and – for some bizarre reason – their horses occupied the ground floor. This was because there was some slight possibility that the horses would appreciate the splendid architecture, according to the grim joke doing the rounds of the town at the time. But no-one was laughing when the full extent of the destruction was eventually revealed. The silk covered walls upstairs had been slashed and gouged, magnificent plasterwork ceilings crumbling and blackened and the parquet floors – the work of master craftsman from France – hacked up for firewood. Downstairs, horse dung had been left to rot throughout the rooms. The stench was unbearable.

For many years afterwards, the palace remained derelict. But now, like much of Pápa, it is being restored, if not to its former glory, at least as far as funds will stretch. Billboards around town are already advertising winter concerts in the ballroom and art exhibitions in the library.

Unlike the house, much of the garden remains untouched though as I walk down the cracked path in the direction of the station, I see the unmistakable outline of a rose garden. Amid the weeds and ivy, rose bushes planted in a circle are laden with red and white roses. On closer inspection further along the path, a pile of pale stones reveals an ancient archway, two moss-covered urns and an elaborately carved marble bench. Heading towards the gate leading out onto the street, I become aware of the most amazing scent. Out of nowhere, strong and almost overpowering. I turn the corner and there it is – the famous Acacia Walk! The path is flanked by gnarled trees planted symmetrically on either side. Thick clusters of creamy white lilac blossom, so heavy they bend the branches of the trees to form a canopy over my head, almost obscuring the sky. I had completely forgotten about this but suddenly I hear my mother's voice. "Like thick lace…And the scent…! I will never forget the scent!"

Years ago, my parents planted an acacia tree at our weekender in the Southern Highlands. Despite careful tending and much encouragement, it did not produce a single bud for a long time. Then one weekend when we were staying there together, my mother and I undertook our regular inspection of the garden and were rewarded by a mass of blossoms. Delighted, my mother pulled a branch down towards her and buried her face in it. For a long moment, she inhaled the sweetness. When she looked up, I saw tears in her eyes. She told me about the Acacia Walk. How the girls had special permission to go into that part of the garden, sit under the trees and pick the blossoms to decorate the convent. Armfuls of fragrant blossom. Unaccustomed freedom. Carefree girls in that last happy summer.

"I'll show it to you one day," my mother promised.

She never did. This promise, like so many others stolen by the cancer that claimed her. But I'm here at last standing under the canopy. Remembering. And like her, I'm crying as I bury my face in the blossoms. It's been a wonderful day. I came to Pápa for an echo of my mother only to be blessed with her scent as well.

CHAPTER 5
My Father's Piano

My parents were a great example of the old saying – opposites attract. My mother loved to cook while my father was not interested in food. When I was a child, I often wondered whether she found it difficult to live with a man whose knee-jerk response even before the first morsel of food hit his plate was, "Don't give me that much!"

She seemed to take it in her stride and the queue of appreciative people lining up to savour and rave about her cooking must have made up for her husband's lack of enthusiasm. And as the years went on, my father became increasingly fond of her delicious cakes and desserts. Munching happily on chocolate torte or lemon-curd pie, he usually saved his, "Not that much!" protest for vegetables.

It was in the area of musical ability however that my parents were totally mismatched. My mother was – and there is no polite way to say this – tone deaf. She always claimed she 'enjoyed' music, but the truth was that concerts, recitals and operas represented a relaxing break from her busy life. An opportunity to sit comfortably and think.

For my father, music was the stuff of life. Like both his parents and older brother, he was musically gifted. Uncle Robert was somewhat of a child prodigy back in his home town Győr.

He pretty much taught himself to play the piano when he was a toddler and commencing music lessons at the advanced age of five, stunned his teachers with his natural ability. Robert was blessed with many talents. He spoke five languages fluently, he drew and painted well and was a gifted writer but unfortunately, he never seemed able to decide which of this abundance of riches he should focus on. Sadly, in the end, he didn't focus on any.

World War II destroyed what could have been a sterling musical career and he abandoned the piano. Some years later in Australia, he became enamoured with the Classical guitar and especially the music of Spanish virtuoso Andres Segovia. He taught himself to play and within a few years became a sought-after teacher of this difficult instrument.

My grandmother had a beautiful alto singing voice and took lessons in her youth while my grandfather, although he lacked any formal training, was also very musical. My father – younger than his brother by two years and always feeling somewhat overshadowed by his talented sibling – had a fine baritone voice and played the piano beautifully. But his greatest gift was that of a 'perfect ear' for music. He only had to hear a piece once or twice before he could play it faultlessly on the piano. He could whistle entire symphonies from memory. He could also – as is often the case for those with this gift – whistle just ever so slightly 'off key'.

During my childhood, I often remember he and my grandfather working together on some DIY Project. When dad wanted to enliven proceedings, he would begin to whistle a slightly off-key rendition of an old favourite like the *Blue Danube*. Refusing to rise to the bait, my grandfather gritted his teeth and kept working – the notes jarring painfully on his ear. By about verse three however, he couldn't stand it any longer and yelled at his son to shut up. All wounded innocence, dad would oblige, adding, "But I thought you liked music?" Once my grandfather became so agitated, he threw a hammer at the whistler. Luckily his aim was as off-kilter as the tune and the projectile hit the wall. The resulting dent called for some creative explaining to my grandmother and mother.

Back in Hungary, the family piano (an exquisite walnut upright) was the only precious heirloom to survive the war. During the bombing raids of Győr in 1941 and 1942, many houses around them were destroyed. Miraculously, only the back of their house and the cellar suffered this fate. Even more miraculously, the cellar was not occupied at the time. My grandfather went off to war at the end of 1941 and did not return until 1945. My grandmother looked after her two young boys as best she could but before he left, my grandfather rigged up their cellar as an air-raid shelter. On those terrifying nights, while American and English bombers zoomed overhead dropping their deadly cargo, the little group huddled together behind the furniture they had stored there in an attempt to preserve the family pieces. It didn't work. The cellar exploded in a ball of flame from a stray bomb discarded when the planes headed for home. My grandmother and the boys had managed to scramble out only seconds earlier.

With the cellar gone, they had no option but to stay in the house during the air-raids. In desperation they sheltered under the piano, which was too heavy to move down into the cellar. The largest piece of furniture they still possessed and might therefore afford some protection, or as my grandmother once put it, "It was so very beautiful I just couldn't imagine anyone wanting to bomb it!" Questionable logic but it did the trick.

When the bombing raids eventually ended, the unfortunate piano faced an even greater danger – hunger. By 1943, food in

Hungarian cities was becoming scarce. Whatever was available was brought in from the countryside and enormously expensive. With such severe shortages of everything, money was a useless commodity. Barter became the norm. My grandmother began to trade whatever she could find to keep her boys fed. So many precious mementoes were lost forever. Her jewellery went first – every necklace, bracelet, earing and ring except her wedding ring. This was soon followed by the family silver – a large heavily embossed tray, soup tureens and serving platters. The cutlery setting. A punch-bowl that had been a precious wedding present. This put bread and sometimes even a little meat on the table and they still had a vegetable garden that grew a few things – mostly swedes, potatoes and carrots. The numerous fruit trees in their orchard had given up the ghost after being scorched by incendiaries but just occasionally, there might be an apple or two or even a peach to supplement the black-market bread.

The silver and porcelain saw them through 1943 and into 1944. Then it was time for the books, paintings, tapestries and any piece of furniture that had not met its fiery end down in the cellar. Then the four fur coats, Russian sable hats and mufflers…

Family heirlooms were not the only things lost to the war. Like their entire generation, the war robbed her sons of their childhood. At 17, Robert was conscripted into the forced labour corps and spent his days digging trenches for the soldiers and his nights snatching what sleep he could in barracks close – so terribly close – to the front line. His mother rarely saw him. Fear that he would be killed in the final months of the war lay heavily on her heart even as hunger assailed her stomach.

My father was only 15. She protected him as much as she could from the devastation, even insisting he went to school every day, although this took him away from her into the city.

But there was nothing she could do to completely shield him from the horror all around. She would never forget his haunted eyes the night he returned home after spending hours pulling corpses out of the smoking ruins of the local hospital. A stray bomb had flattened the Children's Ward. The rescue effort, mounted by the students and teachers from the high school next door, yielded only tiny bodies, blackened and disfigured beyond recognition.

By the beginning of 1945, my grandmother had bartered almost everything of value in the increasingly desperate struggle to stay alive. The pantry was bare. The rooms denuded of anything worth bartering. Except the piano. It still held pride of place in the otherwise empty sitting room, its pale cream walls bearing only the outline of the pictures, mirrors and tapestries that had hung there for many years. Every so often when things got really desperate, she stood beside the piano, ran her hand across its still gleaming lid, lovingly fondled the brass candleholders and stroked the ivory keys. No-one played it now – it was badly out of tune due to the vibrations of the bombs that had fallen around them. It made perfect sense to barter it. It was very valuable and would keep starvation at bay for a while longer.

But no matter how tempting it was, she just couldn't bring herself to do it. The piano represented the past – her family's past – that now lay in smoking ruins all around her. And even more importantly for this brave, loving mother, the piano represented the future. The future she yearned for. The future she still dreamed of for her sons when this hell on earth finally ended and sanity returned. One day, her little family would sit in this room again in the soft golden twilight, the doors thrown open onto the garden. Her boys would play this piano. Robert, grown to manhood now, his fingers tripping magically across the keys.

And little Otto – lacking his brother's genius but blessed with a sensitivity and depth of feeling rare in one so young. No, it did not matter how hungry or cold they were, the piano remained.

Only hell lasts forever and over the next five months, things did get better. The Russians routed the Nazis and Hungarian soldiers began to come home. My grandfather returned and somehow the family survived the end of the war and arrival of the Russians. In 1948, after the communist take-over, their house was requisitioned by a Russian officer. They took it in their stride, moving into a much smaller house they owned a few kilometres outside the city. The piano made the journey with them and found a new home at the end of the hallway by the back door. The rooms were small, the piano was very large and there was simply nowhere else to put it. With the exuberance of youth, the two boys made a game of it. Whoever entered the house through the back door had to squeeze past the piano but first, they had to improvise a piece of music. They entered into the game with gusto and even visitors took part.

***

When my parents left Hungary, the piano stayed behind – as did almost all their possessions apart from what they could pack into the small green suitcase my father carried and my mother's brown handbag. Several years later, when my grandparents finally received permission to join them, the government gave them 21 days to leave the country and they were only allowed to bring 'personal items' with them. So, my grandmother parted with their beloved piano, selling it for a fraction of its true value to the city's conservatorium. It was one of the hardest things she ever had to do.

When my parents bought their first home in Sydney and furnished it on the smell of an oily rag, they didn't even dream of buying a piano. Or more accurately, while my father may well have dreamed of it, there were other much more pressing needs. Like a refrigerator and a heater.

Over the next years, family finances improved. My parents sold their first home at a handsome profit to fulfil their dream of living near the beach. They bought another house that, while also a deceased estate, actually came with intact walls, floor and a fully functioning roof. At that point, although not in any way flush with funds, my father took the decision that it was high time a piano joined the family. He was the most unassuming and humble of men and would never have justified such an extravagance for himself, but I was nine years old by this stage. Piano lessons were long overdue to ensure that I took my place among the talented musicians in the family.

Sadly, I could have told him from the get-go that this was never going to happen. He clearly had not been paying me much attention. Although I sang in the school choir (everyone did) and had learned to play the recorder (like 95% of the students) when the good fairies assembled to hand out talents and natural abilities at my birth, the one in charge of music must have misplaced her invitation. I was not tone deaf like my mother but neither had I inherited the Lang 'perfect ear/musically gifted' gene.

I took piano lessons for years. I sat exams and passed them. I learned to play *Für Elise* and *Lara's Theme* from *Dr Zhivago* by sight. But I had no spark. No passion. No innate talent. I did it because I was a good obedient little girl who wanted to please her parents. And because my pocket money was directly linked to the number of hours I practiced.

But my father was in his element! Not only could he play the piano again, but he could also 'help' me with my lessons. Unfortunately, his help consisted of sitting in the next room while I painstakingly laboured over yet another difficult new piece – Mozart or Debussy or – my nemesis – Franz Liszt. (Note to piano teachers everywhere – just because your student is Hungarian, Liszt is not 'second nature' as some dopey music-teaching nun once insisted. Nor – heaven forbid – is Bartok!)

Every evening, having completed my regulation 60 minutes bashing away, I was itching to escape but before I made it out the door, my father swept in. Grinning from ear to ear he seated himself at the piano and looked like he really belonged there – a feat I never mastered. "Lovely piece. Lovely piece," he enthused before playing it almost note perfect. I only made the mistake on the first few occasions of asking him when he had learned it. His response of, "Never heard it before! But it's a lovely piece!" depressed me for days.

Most nights after dinner, while my mother watched television or planned the menu for yet another dinner or lunch party, he headed upstairs to the sitting room and played for hours, usually in semi-darkness accompanied by the sound of the ocean beyond the glass doors. In my bedroom next door studying, reading or wallowing in teenage angst, even I had to admit he was talented. While his playing may not have been technically perfect, his sensitive execution more than made up for it. He had a very mixed repertoire – well you do, don't you if you only have to hear any piece once to be able to reproduce it? Ranging from old gypsy tunes, to jazz and Blues to yes – Liszt and Bartok. He also loved Burt Bacharach, Abba, The Beatles and was not above syncopating popular advertising jingles. On warm summer nights, I'd sneak out onto the balcony and lie watching the stars, listening to him play. All the emotion, the love he was incapable of expressing in words pouring out through his fingers.

My parents gave wonderful dinner parties. These had progressed beyond the 'bring building materials and a bottle of cheap red' get-togethers in their first home but they were as noisy and joyous as they had been then. The evenings often culminated in the rendition of old Hungarian folk-songs – my father at the piano, the guests sprawled on armchairs and my mother bustling around making sure everyone's wine glass was filled.

I was at the age where I found my whole family deeply embarrassing and these displays of unseemly behaviour excruciating in the extreme. I was an avid reader, totally in love with English literature, especially the writings of Jane Austen. I dreamed of attending genteel dinner parties, making witty conversation and dancing gracefully with my handsome partner, who, it goes without saying, was a Gentleman of Great Fortune. This noisy Hungarian rabble who invaded our home with alarming regularity was beyond the pale.

Years after moving out of home and getting on with my own life, I was again fortunate enough to attend one of these dinner parties. And I realised how very wrong I had been. These people were inspiring, resourceful, immensely courageous. I ate and laughed and reminisced with them and felt a profound sense of admiration. They had left their homes and their families behind, came to Australia penniless and made worthwhile lives for themselves. They had all established loving families while many had built very successful businesses and forged outstanding careers.

As I watched them becoming tipsy, for a moment I could imagine the young people they had once been. There was M – a slight, grey-headed man. An accountant by profession who after years of working in factories while he re-qualified, now ran his own flourishing firm. Standing next to my father at the piano as they sang together, I had a glimpse of the heroic young man who fought the Russians on the streets of Budapest in 1956 and suffered a bullet to the thigh and two years in jail for his pains. And

G, who lost his entire family during the war – mother, father and sisters wiped out in a bombing raid. But he was also singing, glass of wine in his hand, swaying to the beat, happy and alive. And suddenly, I realised that heroism and courage, grace and gallantry did not only reside in English drawing rooms. I had grown up surrounded by it.

As he grew older, my father developed arthritis and found playing the piano increasingly painful. I don't know when he actually stopped playing but eventually the piano was allowed to get out of tune and became just another piece of furniture. My mother kept silver-framed photos and a vase of flowers on it. But at family gatherings when we congregated in the sitting room before attacking the table groaning with food in the dining room downstairs, my dad would always move his chair to sit next to the piano and drape his arm across it, like the shoulder of an old dear friend. Once while we were trooping downstairs to eat, I turned back and saw him lift the lid, gently touching the keys. I think he missed it dreadfully.

My father died of a massive heart attack when he was only 77. Five years later, we lost my mother to cancer. My brother and I decided to sell the family home – we both had our own homes and families and it was not practical for either of us to uproot to the northern beaches.

We began the heartbreaking, backbreaking task of getting the house ready for sale by doing a major de-clutter and make-over, getting rid of my parent's old fashioned, heavy furniture to embrace the breezy beach resort style the location demanded.

The upstairs sitting room was being converted into a Parents' Retreat with sweeping views of the ocean along one side, a low wide bed and comfortable armchairs. Much as I tried to fit it into this decorating scheme, it was obvious that the piano – large, upright, walnut – stood in the way of these plans. It had to go. Getting the piano into the house originally had been a major undertaking and getting it out was going to be every bit as fraught. As my brother and I sat drinking tea, pondering exactly how we were going to achieve this, I had a distinct impression of my parents looking down on us laughing and thinking, "This will be fun to watch!"

Several years after my parents first acquired the piano, they demolished their existing home and replaced it with a double-storey house with wide balconies to take advantage of the panoramic views. As the building work progressed, it became obvious that it would not take eight but more like twelve months for it to be completed. Christmas was around the corner and my mother was getting antsy. The charm of the tiny cottage we had moved into for the duration had long worn off and she was fed up with not having a proper kitchen. In fact, she had not wanted to demolish the existing house – my father had been the instigator of that plan. After much persuasion, she eventually went along with it, having extracted the solemn promise that, "It will be finished by Christmas!"

Hand on heart, my father promised we would be in by mid-December and assured her that absolutely nothing would go wrong. The builder promised. The tilers and plumbers promised. The electrician promised. The carpenter promised. Unfortunately, the carpenter lied. As well as taking on this job, he has another three jobs going at the same time and effective work-flow management was not one of his strengths. One day in early December, as my father was spending increasing amounts of time arguing with the carpenter and my mother's lips were becoming thinner by the day, disaster struck. Already months behind schedule, the carpenter installed the internal staircase only to discover that it didn't quite fit the space. It sat snugly in its designated position just like it had on the architect's drawings, but it was positioned so close to the front door that when you stepped inside, you fell across the first step.

I don't know what my father said to the carpenter. But my mother said only two words to my father, "By Christmas!" and left the rest to his imagination. Three days later, we all visited the site again. The carpenter proudly threw open the front door. Separated by an acceptable width of flooring, the staircase rose up proudly before us. It seemed perfect – polished timber banisters, wide steps. But my mother was not fooled. She looked at my father and asked "How?"

My father looked at the carpenter who admitted – and he did have the grace to blush, "No landing."

My parents faced an interesting dilemma – a new home by Christmas with a staircase that wasn't designed to be spiral but now was. Or the festive season in a tiny rented cottage where my mother would dole out daily portions of cold shoulder and deadly silence together with the Christmas turkey to my poor father while we waited another month for the new house to be finished. My mother spent half an hour going up and down the offending staircase before announcing that she could live with it. It was reasonably wide and the improvised spiral bit half way up – where the landing should have been – was manageable. My brother and I loved it – like having our own slippery dip just outside our bedrooms. My father – well, I think he was just very relieved.

We moved in by Christmas – 23 December to be exact. Over the next few weeks, all our larger pieces of furniture arrived from storage to be lugged up the spiral stairs by four sweaty men who were desperately wishing they had never accepted the job. Then it was time for the piano. It wasn't even worth trying the stairs.

A crane was hired to lift the piano over the railing onto the upstairs patio from where it could be wheeled into the sitting room through the conveniently positioned sliding doors.

Our new house stood at the end of a short cul-de-sac. The entire street turned out to watch and the whole exercise took on a distinctly carnival atmosphere. My best friend and I sat on the front lawn smiling brightly at the crane driver who was what my daughter would now term 'hot' but who we then described to each other as 'dishy'. My parents stood with several neighbours in the front garden drinking coffee and eating my mother's freshly baked almond shortbread. My brother sat on the fence with his friends and made money. Even at seven years old, he was the most entrepreneurial member of our family and was not about to let such an opportunity slide by. Charging his friends 50 cents to watch, he ran a betting shop for the more adventurous. The odds were 10:1 the piano would hit the patio and be damaged. And 40:1 it would fall from the crane and smash into a thousand pieces.

Sadly for his friends, neither happened and eventually the piano took up its position in the sitting room. The neighbours went home, and the hot/dishy crane driver left, happily carrying a foil wrapped parcel of almond shortbread. My brother went inside to count his illegal earnings and my father headed upstairs. The piano needed major tuning after its crane trip, so he couldn't play it yet, but he sat opposite, glass of wine in hand to welcome it to its new home.

In the intervening decades, the piano had not become any smaller nor had the staircase miraculously grown a landing and my brother and I realised it would have to go down the same way it came up. My brother took on the task of finding a crane company that specialised in piano removal while I faced the even more onerous problem of what to do with it after we got it out of the house.

My brother had never learned the piano. As a child he was far more assertive than I had been and my father's last-ditch attempt at nurturing a musically gifted child ended before it began. He point-blank refused to take lessons and before my father marshalled all his parenting skills for another go at persuasion, my grandfather took my father aside and put paid to the plan. I don't know exactly what words my grandfather used to convey his message but, "Don't bother. My grandson is tone deaf," would probably have been among them. Yup – heredity was having the last laugh. The only musically relevant gene handed down in my immediate family was not the one anyone wanted. My brother and mother shared more than just their lovely wavy hair and optimistic outlook on life. I suspect my father had known all along about his son's affliction but had continued hoping for a miracle.

So, when it came time to decide the fate of the piano, suggesting to my brother that he take it smelt more of desperation than reality. And I really didn't want it in my house. We had room for it and it was beautiful but as a wife and mother, the last thing I wanted was to import another source of guilt into my life. I had more than enough home-grown ones, thanks very much. I didn't need the piano looking at me reproachfully when I got home from work every evening – like our dog when I didn't have time to walk her. I toyed for about 30 seconds with enticing my then 13-year old daughter to embark on lessons, but sanity prevailed. Like me, she loved music – so long as it was played by someone else.

So – one piano – free to a good home.

As the weeks went by, I was tempted to offer money to anyone who would take it. It was such a tragedy – it was a handsome piece and had been greatly loved. To de-clutter the house, we had to get rid of a lot of stuff – clothes, furniture, books, ornaments. Instead of giving these to worthy causes such as St Vincent de Pauls or the Smith Family, I found an organisation that helps recently arrived refugees. My parents had come to Australia as refugees, so it felt right to try to assist other people in the same situation. While donating a piano might be stretching things, I called them again, explained my predicament and asked if they were interested. I offered to foot the removalist fees (not to mention the crane). The lady in charge sounded genuinely sorry she couldn't help but after speaking to her colleague said she would ring me back. A few minutes later, she phoned to tell me of a family they had just taken onto their books. The mother and father had both been music teachers in East Timor but were now working as cleaners in a hospital. The eldest of their three children had been learning the piano since she was four. She had all the makings of a gifted musician but even if they did not need to pay for lessons, there was no way they could afford a piano.

It was a heaven-sent solution.

A few days later, a crane was again backing into the cul-de-sac, closely followed by a removalist's truck. A new group of neighbours and their children watched the delicate operation and although home baked almond short-bread didn't make an appearance, it felt just like old times. Right down to my brother betting the removalist $20 that he couldn't lift the piano off the patio on the first attempt.

I had packed all my long-neglected sheet-music into my old leather music case and included the phone number of the piano tuner who I had already paid to tune it for the new owners. As the removalist's truck drove away from the house and everyone cheered, I felt strangely bereft.

My parents' house sold a few weeks later and I prepared to say goodbye to my childhood. Shortly afterwards, a letter arrived there addressed to me. I opened it. Inside was a note written in a childish hand. "Thank you very much the piano!" Attached to it was a photograph of a little girl about nine years old. Ebony skin, black shiny hair in two thick braids and a gap-tooth smile. She is sitting at my father's piano. Her little hands rest expertly on the keys and she looks completely at ease.

And up in heaven, my father is smiling.

Otto with the younger of his two non-musically gifted children.
Not happy!

CHAPTER 6
Feasts of Christmas Past

As must be obvious by now, food is very important to Hungarians. While this may in part be due to the countless times in our long history when we didn't actually have any, it goes deeper than that. Food is love. Food is how you show someone you care. Food is how you celebrate. Food is also how you prove to all the other women in your immediate circle that you are a better cook than they are. But best not to go into that here.

And there is no greater Food-Fest for Hungarian families than Christmas. In fact, we enjoy it so much we are unable to wait until 25 December to celebrate it. Like much of Europe, we make the night before the focal point of the event.

If you will allow me to put on my theologian's hat for a moment, there is actually a wealth of evidence to suggest that this is biblically accurate. The shepherds were tending their sheep by night. The three wise men used a star to guide them. Rudolph's red nose would never have been such a big deal if Santa was making daytime deliveries. Ok, Rudolph is stretching it theology-wise, but you get my drift. Bright stars, moonbeams, soft velvety darkness punctuated by angelic hosts. Clearly the action at Christmas got underway when the Christ Child was born at night. So, it makes sense to celebrate at night. And Hungarians sure do! Of course, we also celebrate on Christmas Day, but more in a 'let's just keep gorging ourselves and drinking too much' kind of way.

Hungarians haven't outsourced the job to the jolly fat man in red. The Christ Child Himself delivers the presents but as the warm up act on 5 December, we commemorate St Nikolas's Eve. Don't be fooled however – while he may look a bit like Santa, our St Nik is not the merry bringer of goodies. He is a dour taskmaster with a list fetish. Yes, he does wear a red suit and has a long white beard, but he isn't the least bit interested in what presents you want for Christmas. His sole job is to check whether over the past 12 months you have been naughty or nice, although minus the forgiving attitude and jolly Ho Ho Ho.

Accompanied by his elf henchman/Executive Assistant, St Nik arrives armed with an inventory of your past misdemeanours. You get a chance to explain yourself while he listens and frowns and the EA takes notes. Then they leave. (Believe me, it's a laugh a minute!) The next morning, if you did badly at your annual Performance Review, you will find a big lump of coal and a bunch of twigs in the painstakingly polished pair of shoes you left outside the front door the night before. If you were good – you get chocolate. That's it. Chocolate. Hardly worth the polishing, if you ask me. Although no-one ever did.

Clearly, my parents and grandparents shared my opinion. Unwilling to compromise time-honoured tradition, my reward remained chocolate plus – as a warning against complacency – some coal or anything as close to coal as my parents could find in the heat of the moment. But instead of my own tiny shoes, I was permitted to leave out a pair of gum boots to be filled. And they didn't even have to be my own gumboots. Having quickly worked out that my grandfather had by far the biggest feet in the family, I always borrowed his and was rewarded by an impressive confectionary haul while he, poor man, spent the next two weeks dislodging mini Mars Bars, Kit Kats and barbeque starters from the toes of his gardening footwear.

Of course, I never actually got to see old St Nik – my grandmother explained that only very, very naughty children did. My list was compiled, and the interview conducted by my dad standing in for senior management and my mother looking very uncomfortable in the supporting role.

I don't remember when we gave up this charming, life affirming little ritual, but it was probably the year after our dog ate one of the gumboots. As my grandmother always purchased a new pair for my grandfather especially for the occasion, she was pretty miffed.

Although probably not as miffed as my father when he was confronted by the hefty bill. I wish I'd been present when he explained to the vet that the patient needed to be treated for consumption of rubber, chocolate and a briquette.

St Nik's arrival and – even more looked forward to – departure signalled the real lead up to the big day. Woops – night. My father began sourcing the live Christmas tree and untangling the fairy lights and my mother went into *beigli* overdrive.

According to the English translation of The Cuisine of Hungary[1] by George Lang (no relation, but boy can that guy cook!)) a *beiglie* is a, "roulade filled with walnut or poppy-seed… traditionally made at Christmas and Easter". A more accurate description appears in one of the many cookbooks I inherited from my mother. Simply titled 'Cookbook', the subtitle roughly translates as, The Young Wife's Guide to the Kitchen[2].

She found this gem in a second-hand bookshop on one of our first trips back to Hungary in the late 70's. Although by this

---

[1] *The Cuisine of Hungary*: George Lang, Bonanza Books. New York. 1971
[2] *Szakacskonyve*: Vizvari Mariska, Minerva Kiadaz. Budapest 1955

time she knew her way around the kitchen pretty darn well, she loved its olde worlde charm. It had been written as a guide for newly married (and comfortably off) women in the 1920s. As my mother pointed out, had the same book been published when she was a new bride in those grim post-Soviet occupation days, the recipe for Sunday Roast Chicken may well have started with –

Step 1: bribe a corrupt Russian-loving government toady to requisition a chicken for you!

The Young Woman's Guide contained some very sensible down-to-earth advice such as ensuring your cook never allows the stock to boil, always salts the meat before cooking and not after and uses a light touch with the paprika.

In relation to *beiglie*, it admitted, "This is a difficult cake to make well," which massively understates the facts. It should have added, "No, seriously. It's really, really difficult. And if in spite of this clear warning, you decide to go ahead anyway, you have been warned!"

I first attempted to make *beiglie* the Christmas after my mother died. I figured it couldn't be all that tricky. I had watched her countless times turn out perfectly formed logs without so much as breaking a sweat in the December heat. Each year she tried her best to persuade me to actually participate rather than just observe. But I kept saying, "Yes, sure. Next year." as I sneaked chunks of the delicious filling into my mouth when her back was turned. "Next year…" Thinking we had all the time in the world.

Eight months after she died, I put on her big apron, set out her mixing bowls, her rolling pin and her kitchen scales on the bench. It all looked achingly familiar except that the person who actually knew what to do next was missing. Fighting the now all too familiar sense of loss, I took a deep breath, opened The

Guide… and read the instructions. Dear Lord – not only were there about a million ingredients listed but you had to mix and knead and scrape and shape and knead and mix and rest, the dough, not the cook. Sadly. The instructions went on for two pages ending with the prophetic line – "This is a difficult cake to make well." Just in case you hadn't worked that out by this stage.

Staring at the pretty pencil sketch of the finished product, I again heard my mother implore, "Let me teach you. Do it with me. I'll show you how." Wishing with every ounce of my being that I had agreed, I gritted my teeth and set to work. The next hour was downright ugly as I struggled to follow the often-cryptic instructions, including such gems as ,"When the dough is the correct texture, stop kneading." Yes. Thank you. Very helpful.

I almost gave up five minutes into the exercise, but I knew that somewhere in the clouds my mother was watching me, shaking her head and saying, "I told you so!" Pure stubbornness kept me at it until I realised that I remembered quite a lot just from watching her year after year.

Finally, there in front of me lay three walnut logs. Neatly wound, washed in egg glaze and ready to 'rest'. As was I. But before I took to my bed with a cup of herb tea, I marvelled again at my mother's culinary skills. Every Christmas she turned out ten, sometimes twelve, of these long rolls, most of which she wrapped in tin foil, tied with red ribbon and gave away as gifts to appreciative friends and neighbours. Then she did it all again at Easter.

After we had both rested for 45 minutes, the uncooked *beigli* and I confronted each other again. The *beigli* definitely looked more relaxed than I did. In fact, it looked pretty darn good with its glossy, smooth surface. But the biggest test was yet to come. These delicious logs are notorious for cracking open during the baking process. If this happens, it is a culinary catastrophe irrespective of how delicious the finished product may taste. In fact, you don't usually get to find out how it tastes because any self-respecting Hungarian housewife will throw it all out and start again. As far as I remember, this only happened to my mother once. She was inconsolable. She ditched the lot and, swearing the family to secrecy, rushed out to buy the ingredients for another batch. Although this turned out to be perfect, it put a dampener on the whole of Christmas that year.

As there was no way on this earth I was going to go through the painful procedure again (until possibly next year) I consoled myself that it was no big deal if my first attempt cracked. I should be very proud of myself for having done it in the first place and the end result didn't matter all that much. l then spent the next 35 minutes sitting in front of the oven, with sweat pouring down my face chanting, "Don't crack. Don't crack. Please don't crack!"

Miraculously they didn't crack and that afternoon, we sat down to a plate of perfectly formed, walnut swirled, marbled pastry just the right sweetness, uncracked *beigli* slices. I was ridiculously proud of myself and as a reward for the huge amounts of energy I had expended on the task, helped myself to a third slice.

***

The Christmas Eves of my childhood always followed the same pattern. By the time I got up in the morning, the house was buzzing. My mother and grandmother swept, cleaned, dusted and polished everything that wasn't moving. My father and grandfather mowed the lawn, trimmed the edges and generally made sure the garden matched the resplendent perfection of the house. My job was to wash the dog. I suspect this was to keep me out of everyone's way. Neither the dog nor I enjoyed it all that much, but it helped pass the time. The afternoon hours dragged but I knew lift-off was close when my grandfather took me out for a walk.

It had to be a long walk. While we were out, the rest of the family sprang into action. Retrieving the live Christmas tree from under the house where he had stashed it a few days before, my father was permitted to give full rein to his artistic temperament by decorating it. My mother and grandmother flew around laying the table, only occasionally venturing into the sitting room to give helpful suggestions about positioning of stars, tinsel and coloured baubles. Once the tree and table were ready, they all rushed around extracting presents from various hiding places. These were placed under the tree, the lights turned off and the door of the sitting-room firmly shut. At this stage, it was my grandmother's job to let my grandfather know that he could bring me home – by going out and lifting up the flap of the letterbox. For the grownups, this secret signal lent a pleasing air of espionage to the entire proceedings.

While this feverish activity was taking place at home, my grandfather and I were walking around the neighbourhood, taking care to pass the house at regular intervals. I never found it boring because while we walked, my grandfather made up stories for me, on the hoof as it were. They were long, intricate tales featuring brave knights, beautiful princesses, fire-breathing dragons and mysterious castles rising out of the mist. Sometimes they ended a bit abruptly when he spied the uplifted letter box flap but as an indication of his formidable story-telling skills, he always managed to conclude the story in a very satisfactory way. A slain dragon or two, a victorious knight, a swooning princess and a castle alive with music and feasting.

Unfortunately, it all went a bit pear-shaped one year when my grandmother forgot to tend to the letterbox. We walked around for what seemed like hours and probably was, until even my grandfather's imagination was beginning to fray around the edges. Finally, he took the unprecedented decision to return home unsummoned – an act of bravery on par with anything one of his knights could muster up. I remember our arrival was met with cries of, "What took you so long!" I don't remember his response, which is probably just as well.

Every year as I stepped over the threshold, I was greeted with the very welcome news that, "The Christ Child has arrived!" as the sitting room doors were flung open and my father lit the sparklers on the tree. But before I was allowed to launch myself at the pile of presents, I had to sing Silent Night. In German. Or more accurately, my grandmother sang it so beautifully it never failed to bring tears to my grandfather's eyes while I warbled along as best I could. Pure magic. The scent of pine needles. The glow of the sparklers and the sweet strains of *Stille Nacht* will remain with me until the day I die.

After the presents were opened, I rushed off happily to change into the new dress that had been waiting for me under the tree. This was the part of Christmas I loved the most. In an era when straight up and down shifts and short skirts in psychedelic pink, canary yellow or eye-popping lime (and sometimes all three) were the fashion, my grandmother's lovingly crafted ankle length creations evoked another world. Frothy white lace with puffed sleeves and pink rosebuds embroidered around the hem and neck; cream satin trimmed with blue bows on the full skirt and sweet-heart neckline; sleeveless white silk with a wide pink satin sash; pale blue organza overlaid with paler blue chiffon and trimmed with cream ribbons. I was very plain as a child – plump little body, long straight brown hair, dark eyes, olive skin – but as I pirouetted and twirled into the sitting room wearing one of these confections, I felt as close to beautiful as I ever would.

By this time, our dinner guests had arrived, and it was time to attack the mountain of food lying in wait in the dining room. For my mother, this was the whole point of the evening – everything else was just window-dressing. She always cooked enormous quantities of food when they entertained but at Christmas, she pushed the boat out…Right out. Why spend months stuffing a goose like the English did, when you can have much more fun making sure every person around the Christmas table is gorged to breaking point? And the more you loved them – the more you made them eat.

This Love = Quantity of Food Consumed equation went both ways the first Christmas Eve my long-suffering husband joined our family for the celebrations. He was not actually my husband at that point. We were living together – something my mother went to great pains to ignore. When we invited my parents over to see how beautifully we had renovated our bedroom, my father immediately complimented the quality of the paintwork. My mother gave a strangled squeak at the sight of our brand-new queen-sized bed and backed out of the room at such speed she almost toppled down the stairs.

My husband is English, polite and well-mannered as only they can be. I was concerned that in order to redeem himself in my mother's eyes for regularly having his wicked way with her daughter, he would – at some risk to his health – attempt to eat his way into her affections. So, as we drove up to my parents' home that fateful Eve, I issued the stern warning "Pace yourself!"

But he didn't.

He ate five of my mother's famous cheese biscuits while we all drank champagne on the balcony. Then he sampled the freshly roasted chili nuts before we trooped downstairs to take our places at the dining table. In keeping with family tradition, this was covered with my mother's Christmas tablecloth, which boasted red berries, green holly and smack bang in the middle, Santa's large beaming be-whiskered face. Fortunately all this was hidden from view by an avalanche of food – a side of smoked salmon, prawns, oysters, four different types of salad and a huge platter of pickled fish called *acatés hal*. This is a speciality of my father's home city Győr and you either love it or hate it. My to-be husband, Stuart appeared to love it. He loved it so much he had two servings on top of everything else. Then thinking he had done his duty, sat back happily. He smiled rather smugly at me. It hadn't been as much of an ordeal as I had led him to believe.

At that point, I got up to help my mother clear the table. Passing behind him I laid my hand gently on his shoulder and whispered, "And now comes the hot food!" He looked slightly panicky while we loaded up the table again. Chicken breast in apricot sauce. Ham (the size of our Labrador puppy) with a brandy, brown sugar and mustard crust. Tender roast pork stuffed with apples, sultanas and walnuts. Crispy potatoes, cauliflower baked in sour cream, pumpkin mashed with cinnamon and honey, rice with red capsicum and peas.

For the next hour or so, my lovely man outdid himself, eating everything his beaming hostess laid before him. Each delicious, rich, fattening morsel. After a short break while the table was cleared again, and the wine glassed changed, those who were still capable of rational thought loosened their belts another notch.

Then my mother served dessert. No stodgy Christmas pud or mince pies at this meal. She brought out the inevitable *beigli* together with shiny almond filled meringues; champagne jelly solid with berries; a huge fruit plater of mangoes, peaches, apricots and her speciality – hazelnut chocolate log. She always positioned the log right in the middle of the table-cloth, so it looked as if the cake was wearing Santa's hat. While everything my mother cooked was delicious, desserts were always the highlight of her meals. Tonight was no exception. Summoning the fortitude that built the British Empire, Stuart somehow managed to ingest a tiny serving of each one, before slumping back in his chair totally defeated.

It was almost midnight by the time we were in any state to waddle out to our car. Without a word, Stuart handed me the car keys, all the while waving to my parents standing on their porch. I drove down the hill, parked by the beach and we listened to the soothing sound of the waves for a while.

"Can you die of too much food?" he whispered eventually.

Feeling quite replete myself, I was not wholly unsympathetic. But I reminded him that he had been warned. "I told you to pace yourself!"

He groaned. "Pace myself? Oh God. I thought you said, "Brace yourself!"

"But why on earth did you eat so much? Every time my mother offered you something, you took it."

There was a long silence while he struggled with his digestion. "I wanted her to like me," he finally admitted.

"And so gentle reader, I married him," to quote Charlotte Bronte. I knew it was absolutely the right thing to do – I had found a man who was prepared to eat himself into the grave for love.

Recipe for Beigli.

"This is a very difficult recipe to make well!" As you are about to find out!

Ingredients:
1 packet dry yeast (active)

1 heaped tsp caster sugar

¼ cup warm milk

Just over 1/3 cup caster sugar

Approx. ½ cup cold milk

4 cups flour

1/4 teaspoon salt

170- 180 gms softened butter

3 egg yolks

Plus 1 extra egg yolk

1/3 cup icing sugar

Walnut filling:

2 cups finely ground walnuts

½ cup caster sugar

3 tsp very finely grated lemon rind

¼ cup warm water

1/4 cup sultanas – optional

Poppy-seed filling

¾ cups poppy seeds. Put into food processor and blend until smooth paste – but not sticky.

(I told you this would challenging!)

3 tablespoons brown sugar

1 teaspoon very finely grated lemon rind

Runny honey or softened jam – about 2 ½ tablespoons. (When the mixture is ready, taste it to make sure its sweet enough. If not – add more honey or jam)

Method

- Dissolve the yeast and heaped teaspoon caster sugar in the warm milk (first 3 ingredients.) Set aside until foamy. About 20 minutes.

- In a large bowl, combine the rest of the caster sugar, sifted flour and salt. Rub in the butter until it resembles breadcrumbs. Then mix the whole lot together until it is slightly sticky. But no too sticky.

- (I know - this instruction is not helpful. By about now – you will be regretting embarking on this adventure.)

- Make a well in the centre of the dough and add 3 egg yolks. Mix well. Then add foamy yeast mixture.

- Mix it all in until it forms a smooth ball.

- Cover with a tea towel and leave in a warm place to rise. Around 2 to 2 ½ hrs. It should double in size.

- While this is happening, make the fillings.

- Combine all the ingredients for the walnut filling and simmer very gently in a large saucepan for about 10 minutes. This is to blend the flavours – keep stirring. Be careful - it can easily burn.

- Do the same with the poppy-seed mixture.

- Cool both mixtures.

Make the logs:
- Divide the dough into 2.

- Roll each out on a floured board – should be about 30cm x 45 cm. Spread the cooled walnut filling over one piece – leaving a border of about 2 ½ cm all around. Turn all the edges over so the filling does not ooze out.

- Very gently – start rolling the **long side** into a tight log, making sure the ends are tucked in and the long join is on the bottom. Glaze top and sides with the extra beaten egg yolk.

- Do the same with the poppyseed. Leave both to rest for about 20 minutes. Using a sharp fork, pierce each log a few times down its length. This is so it does not crack while cooking. But – no promises!

- Preheat oven to 170C and bake for about 30 minutes. Depending on the density of the pastry, it could take as long as 45 minutes. But check after 30. It must NOT burn. It should NOT crack.

- When cooked, leave to cool completely, then with a very sharp knife, cut into slices on the diagonal. Dust with icing sugar.

- And feel very proud you have managed to make this fiendishly tricky but traditionally Hungarian cake!

CHAPTER 7
Student Life

While my parents' many friends and neighbours happily enjoyed the fruits of my mother's labours, I was in my late teens before I felt comfortable sharing my culinary heritage with my own buddies. The difference between what we ate at home and what everyone else served up was simply too vast.

When I started school in the 1960s, Australian cuisine had not yet evolved into the delicious melting pot of today. I'm really sorry but there is no way to say this without sounding rude – on the whole, Australian cooking was boring, uninspired and bland. Occasionally, it was pretty darn awful. Or that's how it seemed to me, indulged as I was by two exceptional cooks.

My grandparents lived with us until I was 10 years old and my mother and grandmother took turns cooking dinner, vying every night to outdo each other. Even after my grandparents purchased their own home, I spent every weekend with them and the fierce competition continued, although more in a guerrilla-warfare kind of way. On Sunday nights, my mother quizzed me on what my grandmother had cooked over the weekend and would then proceed to cook exactly the same things during the week. If I was being kind, I would put it down to coincidence but I'm pretty sure it wasn't. It did however ensure that even on the most ordinary day, my meals were unfailingly delicious.

That not everyone ate like we did was brought home to me the first time I was invited to stay for a meal after a play-date with an Australian school friend when I was about seven years old. My mother was confused by the invitation –'Stay for tea at 6.30' in the evening seemed a bit strange. My parents and grand-parents rarely drank tea. When they did, they had it in the morning with lemon or occasionally late at night, laced with rum after a particularly challenging day. But she sent me off with the promise of a lovely dinner when I got home.

Although I don't remember the actual play-date, the meal that followed remains forever etched on my psyche. As soon as I joined the family at the table, I realised that 'Tea' meant dinner. I was starving by this time so that was fine by me. But my enthusiasm quickly turned to horror when I was presented with a plate featuring two strange bits of blackened meat. These turned out to be lamb chops. In Hungary, lamb had always been considered 'peasant food'. Neither my mother nor grandmother ever cooked it so this was not a promising start. Next to this alien source of protein sat a large spoonful of shrivelled up green peas and another of greyish mashed potato. It all looked awful and tasted worse. The peas were bullet hard, the mash lumpy and watery and the chops – the chops! In an impressive display of alchemy, my hostess had somehow managed to burn the meat to a crisp on the outside while leaving the inside raw. While the rest of the family ate, I watched blood ooze onto my plate and tried not to be sick.

An interminable time later, the plates were cleared. If my friend's mother wondered why mine remained untouched, she kept it to herself and announced we had, "A very special treat!" This was more like it. I sat up happily, ready for chocolate mousse, strawberry meringue or maybe even my favourite – lemon curd tart? A bowl of something bright red, shiny and weirdly transparent appeared before me. My friend exclaimed excitedly, "Yum, strawberry jelly!" and tucked in. I pushed at the lump with my spoon. It wobbled alarmingly and tried to push back. Never in my life had I eaten food that actually moved! I was not about to start now and much to the consternation of everyone else, I burst into tears. I think word quickly went around the schoolyard that asking me over for a meal was not a rewarding experience and I don't recall being invited again until I was in high school. Even now many years later, I feel guilty about my behaviour – the family had been so kind and welcoming and I had blown it badly.

But if I considered the food eaten by my schoolmates challenging, they returned the compliment in spades. When I first started school, I found it a profoundly stressful, frightening place. I felt different. Let's face it – I was different. Even my name made me stand out like a sore thumb. Every roll-call the teacher skipped lightly through the plethora of Susans, Debbies, Kerrys, Wendys and Marys only to come to a screeching halt when confronted by Gab Ri Ell La. A few teachers didn't even bother getting the pronunciation right and called out Gabriel while I prayed for the ground to swallow me up or for the courage to correct them.

This mutilation of my name went on throughout primary school although it did snare me the lead role in the nativity play every single year. Although I wore a white pillowcase and white tights like all the other angels, as the Angel Gabriel my wings were significantly larger, I had a much bigger halo and even my very own line, "Behold, the baby Jesus!" It was but a small consolation.

If roll call was bad, lunchtime was torture. We all had to sit together. There was nowhere to hide when each child opened their lunchbox to reveal vegemite sandwiches, cheese and tomato sandwiches or the trendiest of the lot in those carefree pre-anaphylactic days – peanut butter sandwiches. That is, every child except me. I would be confronted by ham and cucumber sandwiches or a bread-roll carefully spread with pate and cheese or a crispy fried chicken drumstick wrapped in foil, accompanied by cherry tomatoes. But the worst – the absolute worst – were salami sandwiches. Even if I managed a quick disappearing act with the offending food, the smell wafted and lingered. Some kids laughed. Others pulled faces and teased me while I tried not to cry.

One miraculous day when I was again suffering the torments of the salami and bracing myself for the inevitable reactions, something wonderful happened. Louise was one of the popular group. A golden girl blessed with long blond hair, blue eyes and peanut butter sandwiches. She came over to me and said, "Wow! Salami! Can I have a bite?" I gave her the entire sandwich, together with my heart. After that, although my classmates were not exactly lining up to share my lunch, the teasing died down and I spent the rest of the year fantasising about being Best Friends with Louise. Sadly, it was not to be. She was always kind and friendly and totally out of my league. I remember her fondly to this day and pray that life has been kind to her.

The next decade marked the influx of ethnic restaurants that transformed Sydney into a sophisticated foodie haven – Italian, French, Greek, Vietnamese. There were even a few Hungarian restaurants – including the atmospheric Gap Tavern overlooking the sheer cliffs of Watsons Bay. This quirky little place, serving delicious local specialities washed down by amazing wine, was responsible for many near-fatal hangovers within the Hungarian community, including my very first on my 18th birthday. In shaky, almost indecipherable writing, my diary entry the next day ponders the eternal question, "Exactly how sick do you have to feel before you actually die!!??"

As my parents' circle of friends expanded around this time to include many Australian families, they were also exposed to new food experiences. Before long, my mother's slow roasted lamb shoulder with garlic and rosemary or her lamb shanks in red wine, were popular features of her dinner parties, while champagne jelly laden with strawberries became part of her Christmas repertoire. When it first appeared, I comforted myself with the knowledge that her jelly was so replete with berries it was incapable of movement.

My brother's experiences when he started school were quite different to mine. Unlike me, John was a confident and assertive child, something I attribute in no small measure to his growing up unburdened by an unpronounceable Christian name. If salami ever made an appearance in his lunchbox, it was fleeting. As far as I know, for 13 years his school lunch consisted of one vegemite sandwich and one peanut butter sandwich. White bread. Thick butter. No crusts. He had an enormous circle of friends and ate meals at their homes regularly, wolfing down lamb chops and jelly, probably simultaneously. My mother baked every day and John took her cakes and slices to school to share with friends, thus ensuring his popularity. She was never happier than when John lobbed home accompanied by half the soccer team every Saturday after the game. For hours afterwards, the house smelt of mud, wet jerseys and sweaty adolescent boys, with a faint undertone of chocolate cake.

In fact, so great was the change in Australian society over this period that by the time I got to university, being 'foreign'" was no longer a cause for embarrassment. It made me slightly exotic, somewhat interesting or so I liked to fantasize, though probably erroneously. In any event, even if my university buddies were not overly interested in me, they found my mother's cooking fascinating in the extreme. This was especially the case after I moved into college where we were starving much of the time, not because there wasn't any food but because the food was indescribably awful.

As all students do, we regularly pondered the deeper issues of life. Does God really exist? What is my life-purpose? How can I make that really cute boy in (fill in the class) notice me? But the most incomprehensible question of all remained – how can they make college food taste so utterly vile? We knew the fault did not lie with the raw ingredients. We had watched the huge trucks doing their early morning deliveries – fruit, vegetables, meat, dairy products – all looking perfectly normal. But once inside that shiny commercial kitchen, something malevolent and evil descended, rendering the meals inedible.

In desperation, we wrote an 'Open Letter from the Students to the University'. After carefully outlining the issue, we complained in the strongest language we could muster including a high achieving law student's contribution – *cibum gustat faecem*, which as you may have guessed, was not a compliment. Some creative souls even snuck into the dining room late one night and strung up a large banner proclaiming, "Food prepared here is untouched by human hands. The chef is a gorilla!" Although the university carried out a full investigation, its main concern seemed to be centred on OH & S issues. Had the handyman's workshop been left unlocked overnight, thereby facilitating the 'borrowing' of the ladder? But nothing was done about the disgusting food.

I really don't know how we would have survived if it had not been for my mother. At least twice each month, a group of us would 'just happen to be in the neighbourhood' and pop in for a visit. Always around dinner time. The university was 35 km from my home so this was a stretch. My mother never questioned this and happily flew around the kitchen dishing up a feast. Her well-stocked freezer came into its own and soon we were sitting down to an ambrosial meal of chicken paprika, beef stroganoff, roast chicken, pork chops or whatever happened to be on the menu. And the numbers never fazed her – ten ravenous students got fed as rapidly and as generously as two. She always seemed genuinely delighted we had taken the trouble to come by and never let us leave without giving a foil wrapped parcel to each guest, thereby enshrining herself forever in their collective hearts. On alternate weeks, whenever I went home for a night or two, she always sent me back to college with numerous 'Bundles from Mrs Lang', as her offerings were lovingly known. On the one occasion when I accidently left these behind, my friends had no hesitation in shoving me onto the next bus to go back home and remedy the oversight.

Although my mother's culinary contribution was unfailingly generous, it didn't solve the problem. In fact, it may have made it worse. Remembering her succulent roasts while sitting in the dining hall confronted by a grey slab of something bovine was enough to reduce many of us to tears. Unable to stomach the – and I use the expression loosely – food – we eventually surrendered to a diet of 'Hamburgers with the Lot' and hot chips from the local Greasy Joe's, supplemented by shortbread cream biscuits and cheesecake. The results were not pretty, especially for us girls, who began to resemble Tele-Tubbies. Drastic action was called for and at the end of the year, many of us voted with our feet and 'went flatting', as it was called in those days. Having found a large five-bedroom house within walking distance to the university, four girlfriends and I spent three months over the summer vacation making it fit for human occupation before moving in. It was all terribly exciting. Independence at last! Adulthood, here we come!

In the first flush of enthusiasm, we drew up a weekly cooking roster. Designed and illustrated by the two architecture students, its wording as precise and unambiguous as two law students could make it, the roster was a masterpiece of design and precision. The roster factored exams into our cooking duties (if you had an exam, you were off the hook for 2 weeks prior), major assignments (one week off) and even 'Miscellaneous Mishaps' – where the not-having-to-cook-period was to be negotiated with the group based on the severity of the event. These mishaps inevitably turned out to be affairs of the heart gone horribly wrong. As we were all constantly mired in these, we eventually eliminated this category.

Unfortunately, the one thing the roster had not taken into account was that none of us had ever learnt to cook! But fortunately, we had all learned to read. Armed with that Aussie icon – *The Australian Women's Weekly Cookbook*, we managed to feed ourselves. Our meals usually featuring mince in its many iterations. If it wasn't exactly haute cuisine, at least it was edible. About 80% of the time, anyway.

Back on the northern beaches, my mother fretted constantly about my welfare. In true Hungarian-mother fashion, her main concern centred on food. "What will you eat?" "How will you feed yourself?" Strangely, she hadn't voiced these concerns when I was living in at university, where starvation, or at least malnutrition, really had loomed large.

When I raised this inconsistency with my father, he blamed the Russians. In my father's unshakable opinion, THE RUSSIANS – by which he meant Russia's invasion of Hungary in 1948 and again in 1956 (just in case the West missed it the first time) – was responsible for just about everything that was bad or unfair or unjust in his life and the lives of those he loved. He never missed a chance to remind us of this and he certainly wasn't about to let this opportunity slip past.

"You must understand," he explained in his thoughtful way, "Your mother didn't go to university. Because of THE RUSSIANS! THE RUSSIANS prevented her from finishing her education and she has always regretted it.

"So, she thinks university is a wonderful place," he continued, visibly warming to his theme. "She thinks everything about university is wonderful. The teaching is wonderful! The life of a student is wonderful! The..." At this point, he trailed off. He could see from my expression that asserting my mother was so deluded as to think university food was anything other than dire was taking the whole Russian-Blaming-Thing a touch too far.

Ever practical however, my mother did more than just worry. She began to 'happen to be in the neighbourhood so thought we would call in'. My parents had many friends in the eastern suburbs and dinner parties were still a weekly event so this was not an obvious fib and to give them credit, they usually arrived close-ish to dinner party kick-off time. I was not fooled but having spent the past year regularly dropping in on my parents with a carload of ravenous friends, explaining the round trip of some 70km as 'just passing by...' I wasn't in a particularly strong position to raise logistical issues.

Their visits never lasted long. While my father surreptitiously inspected the electrical wiring for defects and jumped up and down on the floorboards to check for termites, my mother headed straight for the kitchen to satisfy herself that we were eating properly.

Appearing totally focused on the conversation she was having with whoever happened to be home, she would cast her steely gaze around – rapidly taking in the contents of the fruit-bowl and the pantry before sort of casually strolling over to the refrigerator and opening it. Finally satisfied that her daughter and friends could keep scurvy at bay for another week, she handed over the large cake she had made for us. The cake really blew the 'just in the neighbourhood' gig wide open but we were not about to mention this in case she stopped bringing it. I was usually the only one available to escort my parents out as the other girls were already busy stuffing themselves with the baked delight. A quick inspection of the rose bushes by the front door, execution of any stray thrips between finger and thumb, a slam of car doors and they were gone. Until the following week. I would have been mortified if my housemates had not looked forward to the intrusion so much. The cakes were always absolutely delicious.

I was sharing the house with two architecture students, an optometry student and a fellow law student so it was, by any measure, a pretty creative household. Just how creative, I was to discover a few months after we moved in. Unbeknown to me, the girls had planned a little entertainment to liven up the afternoon by playing on my mother's worst fears — that we were indeed starving.

In anticipation of my parents' visit, they cleared all the fruit from the fruit bowl, took every single thing out of the pantry except for a solitary tin of baked beans and emptied the fridge, leaving only a wilted lettuce leaf, a half-eaten apple and a small wedge of hard cheese sitting pathetically on the middle shelf.

My parents arrived and the ritual unfolded. I really wasn't paying much attention and didn't notice that all my flat-mates were at home for once so when my mother did her kitchen inspection, there were five of us in attendance. My mother frowned when she saw the empty fruit bowl. The bare shelves of the pantry caused a sharp intake of breath. The brightly lit cavern of the refrigerator's interior made her gasp as if in pain. I didn't have the vaguest idea what was going on but the other girls were enjoying the show immensely. It was going beautifully to plan. All that was left now was for them to explain and we would have a good laugh together.

Struggling to assume expressions that combined hunger, bravery and resignation in equal measure, they prepared to let us in on the joke. But my mother wasn't hanging around for explanations. This was far too serious. Without even stopping to put down the cake, she grabbed my perplexed father. The front door slammed and a few seconds later, we heard them drive off.

Feeling guilty, the girls confessed and then retreated to their rooms while I sat in the dining room and wondered how to contact my parents. I wanted to make sure my mother was ok. I wanted to apologise. I wanted to stand by looking thoroughly disapproving while every single one of my flatmates grovelled into the phone. Most of all, I really wanted to get that cake back. I hoped it was chocolate – my favourite. I was hungry and, judging by the state of the fridge, dinner was looking very uncertain.

But this was the 1970s – long before mobile phones ensured that you could contact anyone anywhere anytime. It would not be easy to track them down. I mentally began to run through the long list of my parents' friends trying to pinpoint the location of tonight's dinner party so I could look up the phone number. Sometime later, I was just heaving the N to Z volume of the telephone directory onto my lap when the prodigal parents reappeared at the front door.

My mother looked like a woman on a mission. My father looked like a man who was obeying instructions. But more than anything, they both resembled camels setting out to cross the Gobi Desert as they staggered across the threshold weighed down by carrier bags. We all rushed to help but they ignored us and made straight for the kitchen. There, without so much as, "Hello," my mother unloaded fruit into the fruit-bowl and meat, milk, cheese and butter into the refrigerator while the remaining shopping bags spilled out groceries and a paddock's load of vegetables onto the kitchen table. My father leant against the doorway and watched in quiet amusement. I was very pleased to see he was holding the tin containing the cake.

It was no good trying to stop her or help her so we just all stood around and waited. I think the other girls found my mother's ferocious energy more than a little scary and I knew better than to interfere. When she had finished, she stepped back and surveyed the bulging refrigerator with obvious satisfaction. She smiled happily at us before instructing, "Now…eat!"

Dispensing random hugs and kisses to whoever was within reach, she made for the front door. "We are late for dinner," she explained while we followed behind, stammering apologies and thank yous in her slip-stream.

"Don't apologise!" she laughed. "Ever since you all moved in, I've wanted to go out and stock you up. With real food.

"But I couldn't because you would have thought I was interfering. But of course, now that you are starving… I can!"

With my parents and brother – around the time I 'went flatting'.

Not just a suitcase. It was the portal to a new world.

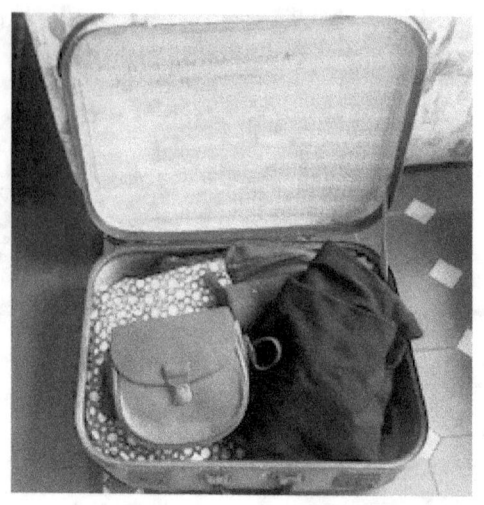

Inside the Suitcase

Otto and Helen. . He could do a mean tango! Waltz. Foxtrot…

CHAPTER 8
The Suitcase

Some families have skeletons in their cupboards. We had a suitcase in our garage. And like the proverbial skeleton, this suitcase defines our family and made us who we are.

Our suitcase was made of heavy cardboard covered in a green check print. It had a sturdy leather handle, leather patches on its four corners and a lining of pale brown striped silk. It did not look at all remarkable. But it was. It did not look like the portal to a new world or the gateway to a new life. But that is exactly what it had been.

I came upon the suitcase when we were preparing my childhood home for sale after my mother died. Although the house itself was not particularly large, the garage was enormous. Originally built to accommodate two sizable cars plus lots of storage, as the years passed, the car component all but disappeared as the storage aspect took over. By this time, there was barely room for my mother's little red car amid the piles of keepsakes, mementoes and those 'just in case' things that had accumulated. My parents were not hoarders – they were merely products of their tumultuous past, when possessions could be confiscated, and precious heirlooms taken away at the whim of others. While we regularly used to quip that my mother 'always cooked like the Russian army was just over the next hill and you didn't know where your next meal was coming from!' it wasn't really a joke. Having experienced exactly this, it affected how she lived the rest of her life.

Now my brother and I toiled away mucking out the garage, trying to subsume our grief beneath piles of stuff. It was hard work heaving the boxes out of the enormous wardrobes that lined the walls, unpacking the contents and revisiting the past. We found at least ten boxes of our old schoolbooks. Mine were carefully covered in regulation clear heavy plastic – such a chore every January – and appeared loved and well cared for even after all this time. My brother's books were either dog-eared, ripped and scruffy or looked brand new, as if they had never been opened. Which may have been the case.

Like our schoolbooks, many of the other boxes reflected our different personalities. Numerous pairs of my brother's soccer boots – from the first tiny bright red pair all the way up to clodhoppers you could almost set out to sea in. Roller skates, rugby balls, surfing paraphernalia, fitness magazines, a chest extender…

My half of the wardrobe was jammed with books, ranging from Enid Blyton's *Famous Five Go on Holidays* to Machiavelli's *The Prince* and two sets of *The Complete Shakespeare*. And pile after pile of clothes including my senior high school uniform, the skirt so miniscule as to be almost irrelevant. Long party dresses lay folded beside elaborate costumes I had worn in school plays. They all came tumbling out in a colourful frothy mass of fabric that smelled faintly of mothballs and very strongly of the past.

By this stage, my husband and daughter had joined us. Soon we were shrieking with laughter as Amelia pranced around amid the clutter wearing my old debutante gown. Even though the lace was yellowed with age it was still exquisitely beautiful. The last dress my grandmother ever made me – intricate roses embroidered on the bodice and a wide circular train.

In the other corner of the garage, I tried without success to squeeze myself into the pale blue silk creation I had worn in my Year 11 school play, lamenting the loss of my promising acting career almost as much as my 25-inch waist.

Like excavating the ancient city of Troy – each tier revealed a different civilisation and my parents' memories lay beneath the layers belonging to their children. Old theatre, concert and opera programs, boxes of recipes my mother had torn from magazines over the years, ski jackets and pants, gardening implements. A big box of camping gear from their wonderful adventure when, much to the consternation and unconcealed disapproval of their two adult children, my parents (then in their early sixties) bought a campervan and set off to explore Australia. They had a glorious time touring around for eight months and returned fit, tanned and looking ten years younger with a wealth of funny stories, four gold nuggets from Broken Hill and an address book full of new friends.

Admitting that I had completely forgotten this episode, I showed the primus stove (sadly rusted now) and other camping bits and pieces to my brother. By the time my parents set off, I had been living away from home for years, but my brother had just turned 18 and was still very much in residence. Obviously overcome with euphoria at their upcoming odyssey, my parents cast caution to the wind and left him in charge of the house and the dog. That decision was to prove unwise on oh so many levels. My brother remembered it all too clearly.

"The dog ran away the first day," he reminisced fondly. "I borrowed Dad's car to go looking for him and accidently drove into the neighbour's fence. The car was ok, but the fence was a mess, so I had to use all the housekeeping money mum left me to get it fixed."

"I almost starved to death," he admitted sheepishly. "I lived on tinned spaghetti until they returned." Ah, memories!

Then – right at the bottom of the biggest wardrobe – we found the suitcase. The hinges were rusted, and we had to force it open. Neatly folded inside was a dark blue man's winter jacket, heavy woollen pants and a knitted scarf. Beneath these lay a pair of woman's walking shoes and a green knitted coat and skirt. On the very bottom, carefully wrapped in tissue paper was a red and white dress with a lace collar, while a small leather handbag with a long strap was tucked into the corner. I opened the handbag. It smelled musty. The lining came apart when I reached into it and pulled out a tiny bible and a crudely carved wooden crucifix.

Fighting back tears I said to the others, "Mum told me she kept this. These are the clothes they brought with them when they left Hungary. This is the suitcase they carried."

***

It was a well-known fact among their many Sydney friends that my parents always arrived late to any social event. Not embarrassingly late but inevitably well after the designated time. Their inability to arrive on schedule became a standing joke in the group; something to be mentioned while that last bottle of red wine was savoured. After a while this reputation – well-earned though it was – began to annoy my father. The next time they were invited out, he put his foot down. Because he didn't do this very often, (wisely, in my opinion) my mother knew she had better humour him. So she made sure that for once they actually left home with time to spare. They drove across the Harbour Bridge to the party and my father was in high spirits. This time, they would be the very first guests to arrive. In fact, they might even turn up a few minutes early!

As they parked outside the house, my father triumphantly commented that there were no other cars yet in evidence. With a flourish, he rang the doorbell and beamed as his friend opened the door. His friend looked very surprised indeed to see them. But before my father could savour the moment, he noticed the poor man was wearing his dressing gown and slippers. They were definitely early. Extremely early. One whole week early. With typical Hungarian hospitality, their friends abandoned their plans for a relaxing evening, invited them in and fed them but it took my parent's several decades to live this mistake down.

My parents' habitual lateness was totally my mother's fault. She was always dressed and appeared ready to go in plenty of time but then, while my father stood at the front door ready to lock up with the keys already in his hand, his life's companion inevitably found just one more thing she absolutely had to attend to before she could leave. Dad would stand shuffling from foot to foot, whistling to pass the time. Softly at first but as the minutes ticked by and one unpostponable task after another presented itself, his whistling moved past forte towards agitato. Finally, my mother would glide past him, saying impatiently, "Come on. We're late!"

Once in exasperation, my father yelled at her, "Do you realise it's taken you almost as long to get into the bloody car as it did for us to leave Hungary!"

While this was obviously an exaggeration, it is true that when my parents escaped from Hungary in 1956, time was among the many luxuries they didn't possess. They abandoned their old lives and left their home in a matter of hours. When I asked my mother once how they had made the journey, she joked, "Very quickly!" To my question of why they decided to go, my father did a very passable Woody Allen impersonation with his, "As if we had any choice, already?"

Yet they did have a choice. Like most of their friends and relatives, they could have stayed under the Soviet yoke, eking out an existence in that brutal regime. That they chose freedom and were prepared to risk imprisonment, even death, to achieve it speaks volumes about their courage, their faith, their tenacity.

It wasn't meant to turn out like that – the defeat of Hitler was supposed to usher in an era of peace and security. But in the mid-1950s, while much of Europe was recovering from the devastation of war, living conditions in the countries of the Soviet-bloc was dire. For the vast majority of Hungarians, fear remained a daily companion and hunger was always just around the corner. When things got really bad, riots broke out – usually due to shortages of bread and other basics – but these were quickly suppressed. The communist hold on Hungary seemed unbreakable.

Married in 1955, my parents struggled to build a life together although the odds were stacked against them. Given their backgrounds, they were tarnished with the stigma of 'Privilege'. They were classified as Enemies of the People and it was irrelevant that both their families had lost their wealth years before. Apartments, jobs and sometimes even food was reserved for the party faithful and like many of their friends, the young couple faced housing shortages and unemployment. Eventually my father found work in a factory that made parts for tanks. My mother worked in a shop. They lived in a single room. Life was hard and the future unrelentingly bleak.

Then suddenly, everything changed. For a few miraculous days, it really did look as if Hungary could regain her freedom. On 23 October 1956, another spontaneous demonstration erupted in Budapest. It began like all the others and like them, seemed doomed to failure. But within a matter of hours, something shifted. "This one...well it just felt different," my father's friend who took part in it once tried to describe it to me. Greatly encouraged by the recent concessions Poland had managed to wrest out of Stalin's successor Nikita Khrushchev, instead of demanding bread, these demonstrators began to cry out for political freedom. Word quickly spread through the various university campuses located around Budapest. Hundreds of students abandoned their lectures and rushed into the city centre to take part. Suddenly everyone was wondering the same thing – if the Poles could do it, why not the Hungarians?

By evening, many young professionals and tradesmen joined the students. The crowd had grown to over 200,000 participants. Seizing the moment, the leaders drew up a list of concessions. These included general elections by secret ballot, freedom of the press and most significantly, the immediate withdrawal of Russian troops from Hungarian soil. Marching through the wide tree-lined streets of Pest, they held hands and chanted, "Ruski go home! Ruski go home! Go! Go!"

It was no longer a demonstration. In a matter of a few short hours, it had become a revolution. Young men climbed onto the facades of buildings to rip down the hated red Hammer and Sickle flags. When they reached their destination – Heroes' Square – a group of them scaled the 30-metre bronze statue of Stalin and managed to push it over. Erected in 1948, this grotesque insult to Hungarian independence was both the most visible and the most hated sign of the Russian presence. Now Stalin's body lay broken into pieces, his massive head cracked wide open on the footpath. Only his boots and the plinth they stood on remained upright. Amid the cheers of the crowd a student leapt over the rubble, climbed onto the broken statue and recited the famous *Nemzeti Dal* (National Song). Written by

Hungary's greatest patriotic poet Sandor Petőfi and credited with inspiring the 1848 revolution, its call, "Rise up, Hungarian nation!" became once again the people's rally cry.

At this point police arrived and opened fire, killing several demonstrators. They were soon followed by the army, which had been summoned by Erno Gero, the puppet Premier. But more and more of the solders refused to fire on the demonstrators and melted into the crowd. Gero panicked. He imposed martial law across the city and called on the Soviets for reinforcements. Help arrived quickly, and the eerie pre-dawn light was broken by the rumbling of Russian tanks. But still the people refused to back down. They were determined. It was time for the Russians to leave!

Thousands of miles away, the Soviet rulers in the Kremlin realised this was serious – far more serious that the Polish situation three years earlier. The Hungarian no longer sought concessions – they demanded freedom! And as the marchers continued to chant, "Ruski go home," the unimaginable occurred. Tanks and soldiers turned around and left. Not even returning to their barracks just outside the city, they slowly made their way along the highway, through the countryside and into nearby Czechoslovakia.

Back in Budapest, it looked like the people had won. The crowd was hysterical with joy. Students took over the state-controlled radio station, proclaiming that the government would no longer dictate what people listened to. Liberal newspapers sprung up overnight and old political parties, banned since 1945, re-emerged. Free speech had returned to Hungary and everywhere, there was the euphoria of possibility. You could almost taste freedom in the cold autumn air.

Meanwhile just across the Czech border, troops and tanks waited. From the first day of the uprising, the students had appealed to the West – especially to the United States and the United Kingdom – to step in and support them. These two countries continued to send messages replete with congratulations and encouragement but neither President Eisenhower nor Prime Minister Eden had any intention of actively interfering. The UK was too concerned about the emerging crisis in Suez to antagonise the Russians over anything as politically insignificant as this small eastern European country and the US was gearing up for presidential elections. Hungary was on her own against the might of the Soviet Union. Counting on this lack of Western involvement, Khrushchev took a massive gamble and won.

At midnight on 3 November, Soviet tanks crashed across the Hungarian border. By the next day, Budapest was under siege. Desperately, the Hungarians pleaded with the West. "Help us! We beg you! We are dying here! Help us!" Hour after hour the same desperate message poured across the radio waves. But no help came and within days, it was all over. Retribution was swift and terrible – over the next few weeks, thousands of young men were executed, imprisoned or simply disappeared into the brutal prison system.

One hundred and twenty-five kilometres away in Győr, my parents had nervously followed history unfolding. Some of my father's friends were involved in the action in Budapest and he got first-hand reports of the Russian army's initial withdrawal. He shared their jubilation and prayed the miracle would last. But when it all came crashing down, he knew that life was about to get even harder, even more dangerous.

Despite being totally outnumbered, the students in Budapest continued to put up a fierce resistance and during that first week, the Russians were concentrating all their efforts on restoring order on the streets. Many thousands of soldiers who were usually stationed around the country were hastily dispatched to the capital, leaving sections of the Austro-Hungarian borders unpatrolled for the first time since 1948.

Unlike neighbouring Yugoslavia, Austria was not part of the Soviet Bloc. Győr was located exactly half-way between the fighting in Budapest and the freedom of Vienna and although no-one could predict how long the border would remain open, a means of escape suddenly presented itself to my parents. It would be extremely dangerous. They would have to leave everything behind – family, friends, possessions; all that was dear and familiar. There was no time to wait – if they were going to escape, they had to leave immediately.

Petőfi wrote his famous call to arms in 1848 – that pivotal time in Hungary's history when the country's fate hung in the balance. Petőfi challenged his countrymen to act and act quickly; dangerous times called for courage and fortitude. His most famous lines could have been written in 1956.

Itt az idő, most vagy soha! Rabok legyünk vagy szabadok?
Ez a kérdés, válasszatok!

This is the time; it's now or never! Shall we stay slaves, or shall we be free?

This is the question. What is your answer?

Together with some 200,000 of their countrymen, my parents answer was to choose freedom. In less than three hours, they were on their way to the railway station. Maybe it was better that they didn't have more time to prepare? Maybe it was easier not to have time to ponder, to feel, to say lingering goodbyes? My father rushed off to the local food-store to buy whatever provisions he could find for the journey while my mother packed.

They only had one suitcase between them and she crammed their warmest clothes, a spare coat for each of them and underwear into it. The suitcase was small, and they wouldn't have been able to carry much in any event but somehow, she found room for her only "good" dress – red with a white lace collar – and her tiny leather-bound Bible. The size of a matchbox, the Bible had been in my mother's family for years and was given to her on her wedding-day. Inside the lining of the suitcase, she secreted a simple wooden crucifix her father had carved during the war. She packed their identity papers, my father's university qualifications, her wallet, a blue handkerchief and her little silver comb into her handbag. The rest of their important documents went into my father's briefcase, together with what food my father had managed to buy – some salami, two loaves of bread, a little cheese.

They made their way to the train station along a circuitous route – on the way, calling on my father's best friend. But he was not at home and it would be almost 20 years before my father saw him again. Then to my father's parents' home to say goodbye. My grandfather was also away, and my grandmother was alone when her adored younger son told her that he was leaving Hungary, like her older son had managed to do in 1948. This news almost broke her heart. She did not try to stop them – she knew it was the right decision. She didn't cry as she kissed them goodbye and hurried them on their way. But afterwards, she stood sobbing by the gate, watching them disappear down the road. My mother's family lived 40 kilometres on the other side of Győr and all my mother could do was leave a letter for her mother-in-law to post.

My parents hurried across the Raba Bridge to the railway station, hoping to catch the train to the town of Hegeshalom, the closest Hungarian town to the Austrian border. They joined the small crowd already assembled there – mainly single men, small family groups, young married couples – all dressed in their travelling clothes and carrying suitcases, backpacks, brief-cases. Then came the frightening news that the trains were no longer running. That section of track had been blown up by the Russians before they withdrew to Budapest. Still determined to leave and now with no option but to walk, my parents joined four other couples and headed out of Győr on foot.

It took them three days to walk the 60 km to Austria. Or more accurately, it took them three terrible nights because they had to make the journey under cover of darkness. Although the troops who usually guarded the border were now in Budapest, small groups of soldiers regularly patrolled the roads. Their orders were to stop anyone trying to escape and they were not in the least shy about firing their rifles. My parents and their companions hid during the day in the forest and walked through the fields at night but even this was very dangerous – every hour or so, searchlights mounted on trucks scanned the open country. When the searchlights lit up the fields, they dived into the nearest ditch if there was time or lay pressed against the ground and prayed they were not spotted.

Late autumn. Traditionally a time of biting cold and persistent rain and this year was no different. Taking turns to carry the suitcase hour after exhausting, freezing hour, my parents walked on and on; the monotonous rhythm of their footsteps only interrupted by yet another frantic scramble to evade the soldiers. Once they had to stand waist-deep in a muddy river while the searchlight scanned backwards and forwards over their heads. At times the stillness was broken by volleys of gunfire and shouts and screams in the distance.

My mother's hat soaked through with rain and her wavy hair became wringing wet. When it dried, it sat like a dark halo around her head. My father's shoes didn't keep out the rain. His feet froze, and he was very fortunate not to lose his toes to frostbite. The days were more bearable than the nights – they rested in the long hay or on riverbanks, but they were too afraid to fall asleep in case the soldiers came. Night descends early at this time of year and by 4 o'clock it was dark, and they could set off again. They were totally exhausted but there was no time to lose. No-one could predict how long the border would remain unpatrolled. For all they knew, it might already be too late.

I cannot imagine what it must have been like. Not just the uncertainty and the anguish of leaving everything they had ever known and loved behind, but the physical effort involved. The hunger and the cold. On one of my first solo trips back to Hungary, I caught the train to the unpronounceable town of Mosonmagyaróvár about ten kilometres from the boarder at Hegeshalom. I was determined to walk along the side of the road for an hour or so to experience just a little of my parents' journey. It was late November. I lasted ten minutes before the sleet and icy rain forced me to return to the warmth of the railway station.

But there was no going back for that little band. On and on they trudged until they didn't think they could go any further. Then suddenly across the wide expanse of ground, they saw the menacing outline of watchtowers silhouetted against the night sky. With the Austrian boarder stretching in front of them, they had no alternative but to leave the protection of the forest and head into open country. My mother and father held hands and ran towards the watchtowers. Headlights beamed out and almost blinded them. But this time, light meant safety and they stumbled the last 50 metres towards Red Cross vehicles and ambulances and a big red and white banner draped across the trees proclaiming *Willkommen in Österreich!*

Welcome to Austria!

Doctors and nurses greeted them with reassuring words, medical assistance and food. My father's feet were washed and bandaged while, too exhausted to talk, he and my mother sat propped against each other by a roaring fire. Using their suitcase as a table they ate their first proper meal since leaving home. Tin mugs of hot sweet milky coffee – real coffee, not the gritty brown sludge that passed for it in Hungary. Hard boiled eggs, salty ham and thick slices of white bread and butter. For the rest of their lives, they agreed it was the best meal they had ever eaten.

Many years later in Sydney in November 1996, my parents hosted a huge party to celebrate the 40th anniversary of their Hungarian exodus. Over fifty of their friends turned up to the happiest, loudest and most boisterous of their many parties. When my mother had announced that the theme was 'Come As You Were', I offered my unsolicited opinion that it was bound to fail. It was a silly idea. No-one would dress up. Who in their right minds kept clothes for four decades?

Of course, I was quite wrong. Despite the summer heat, the guests all turned up wearing a hilarious assortment of ancient suits, raincoats, dresses, walking shoes, hats and mufflers. Many of them even had the handbags and briefcases they had carried, and one man proudly kept his precious old camera, carefully preserved in its leather case, around his neck the entire night. They ate enormous amounts of my mother's wonderful food, drank never mind how many bottles of wine, beer and palinka and danced into the small hours. Having gone over to help my mother beforehand, I couldn't tear myself away. It was such a treat to watch this brave, resilient band of senior citizens kicking up their heels.

My father decorated the dining room with an old Hungarian flag. Next to it – making an unseasonal appearance – my mother's ANZAC Day Australian flag stood proudly with a large stuffed koala clinging to the flagpole. I don't think I ever heard either of my parents use the now hackneyed word 'multi-culturalism'. I suspect my mother would have mispronounced it if she ever had. But they didn't talk about it because they didn't need to. It simply wasn't an issue for them. They lived it from the first moment they set foot in their new homeland. Lived it graciously, generously, joyously.

In front of this eloquent display of flags, their old suitcase served as a platform for dozens of pre-1956 photographs brought along by the guests. Nursing a glass of champagne, I spent a long time examining them. Those young, earnest faces. Bright, beautiful, full of hope and promise, in spite of the heartbreak and tragedy they had all experienced during the war years and beyond. None of them could possibly have suspected how their lives would turn out or how very far away from Hungary they would end up.

I looked out into the garden where the party was now in full swing. Guests sat or stood around in groups eating and talking amid the loud music. As was usual when they entertained, my father welcomed his guests with Puccini and Mozart and would send them home teary eyed and tipsy with old folk tunes and gypsy violins. Between these musical bookends, crooners such as Andy Williams and Perry Como competed with Beethoven and Wagner.

But just now, a waltz by Franz Lehar was playing and several couples began to dance. I watched my father put down his wineglass and walk over to where my mother was fussing with yet more food on the long table set up under the awning. He was a wonderful dancer – so graceful he made anyone lucky enough to partner him look graceful too. He swept my mother into the dance and they dipped and swayed. As they spun past me, my mother whispered something into his ear and I heard them laughing together. Life was good. They were very blessed, and they knew it.

CHAPTER 9.
Travel Broadens The Mind, The Hips, and The Waistline

Taking advantage of the amnesty offered by the Hungarian government to those who had jumped ship during the horror years, in the mid-1970s, with my brother and me in tow, my mother returned to Hungary for the first time since her long walk across the border in 1956. Having previously refused to grant visas, the communist powers that be suddenly decided to let bygones be bygones and allow the Traitors to return home. 'Traitors'. This is what they actually called them in official publications – something that caused my father's blood-pressure to elevate to dangerous levels whenever he saw the reference. But suddenly all was forgiven. The traitorous ones were graciously invited 'to visit family and reconnect with their roots'.

In reality, the Hungarian government was itching to get its hands-on *valuta* (foreign currency) and how better than by promoting tourism? Many of the people who had chosen to exit stage left pursued by Russians were doing very well in their adopted countries. It was now time for them to return to spend as much of their filthy capitalist lucre as possible, thus sharing their prosperity with the government who had tried its hardest to persecute them.

My father's parents and brother had settled in Sydney, but my mother's entire family remained in Hungary. She missed them dreadfully. Every week crisp blue airmail letters flew across the ocean. Several times a year, parcels of photographs followed, showing my brother and me in school uniform, in sports uniform, in bathing suits, on the beach and – this one still makes me cringe – me in the bath on the day before I started high school. Please – before you yell, 'child abuse' or worse – let me assure you that the only things visible were long wet hair, neck, shoulders and a horrified expression. But to this day I wonder what temporary insanity had unhinged my mother to such a degree.

Before heading off on our big adventure, mum stocked up on presents. Not only the mandatory stuffed koalas and kangaroos, with a few wombats and kookaburras thrown in for good measure, but dozens of pairs of stockings, pantyhose and jeans in a variety of sizes. My query led to a fascinating explanation of the economy of Soviet Bloc countries.

"Every five years, the government decides what things the factories will produce and if something isn't on the list, it isn't available. Unless of course you happen to be well connected, (translated – a member of the Communist Party) or have access to other sources." For several weeks that December/January 'other sources' meant us.

I thought she was joking until some years later, I visited on my own, and realised she was spot on. Watching me unpack my suitcase, my aunt's eyes lit up when she saw a small packet of safety pins. Shyly, diffidently, she asked if I could spare one. As I only had them to cope with 'hem down, no inclination to sew' wardrobe emergencies, I offered her the lot. It turned out that safety pins had not been on the production list in Hungary for a while and were by now pretty much extinct. At the same time, the country had embarked on a population drive, offering young women ridiculously generous incentives for producing more than one child. The fact that a harassed mother struggling to secure a thick cloth nappy (Huggies not yet having crawled across the Iron Curtain) was unlikely to want to repeat this torture with more babies seems not to have occurred to the government. In my humble opinion, unlimited access to jumbo size safety pins would have been a far more effective incentive than 24 months paid maternity leave and a generous Baby Bonus.

A week later in Vienna on a quick visit, I purchased every safety pin I could lay my hands on and upon my return to Hungary, solved this problem for my relatives and friends. For the rest of my stay, as well as the bunch of flowers without which no well brought up young Hungarian lady ever went a'callin, I arrived with 20 safety pins of various sizes, tastefully wrapped in cellophane and tied with a red bow. Several recipients burst into tears. Sometimes I did too, seeing firsthand and finally beginning to comprehend the soul-destroying lunacy of socialism.

But I digress.

For the first trip the three of us took, in between indulging in an orgy of present buying, my mother lectured my brother and me on how we were to behave OVER THERE. Things would be very different OVER THERE but at all times, we were to be complimentary, enthusiastic and polite. We were not to criticise anything OVER THERE. The food might be a bit unfamiliar but – eat whatever is put in front of you! And most importantly – this strict instruction accompanied by much index-finger waving was directed at my eight-year-old brother, "If you must criticise something, speak English!" The family rule until now had been to speak Hungarian when we didn't want others to understand and this new directive confused the poor boy so much, he was rendered mute for the first two days of our visit. But when he did regain his powers of speech, he proceeded to acquire a repertoire of Hungarian swear words of such exquisite pungency that my father almost swerved off the road when his son and heir unleashed them as we drove home from the airport on our return.

My father was not coming with us. He was staying in Sydney, so he and my grandfather could build the long-promised carport. Why someone who had worked 12-hour days for the past eleven months would forgo a trip to Europe to be a builder's labourer to my grandfather – who thought the working day began at 6 am and ended at 7pm, with no time off for good behaviour – remains a mystery to this day. I suspect it was because my parents couldn't afford to fly the entire family back. The trip home was his 40th birthday present to my mother. My brother still travelled half fare and well – I guess I just got lucky.

We left Sydney on a blistering 39-degree day when the landing strips at the airport shimmered like silver foil in the heat. Our transit stop in Frankfurt was a rushed affair. Running through the terminal to our connecting flight, we barely noticed the snow-covered buildings outside. Twenty-eight hours after leaving Sydney, arriving in Vienna – where the mercury was reluctantly nudging minus 2 degrees – felt like landing on the moon.

Even negotiating the few steps from Ausgang to Taxi literally took our breath away. But the taxi was well heated as was the train station at which we were decanted, barely visible above our piles of luggage. Novices at international travel, we had not yet learned to pack lightly. Anyway, hosiery, jeans and stuffed wildlife took up lots of space. I also suspect that – having left

Hungary with a small cardboard suitcase and a handbag – arriving back years later surrounded by bulging leather-goods was my mother's own personal, "Up Yours!" to the hated regime.

Getting into Hungary was not easy. Direct flights to Budapest didn't exist at that time. But because my mother's family lived in Győr – conveniently located mid-way between Vienna and Budapest – we caught the Europe Inter-City Express, which made the 250km journey every day at noon. Two hours later we reached Nickelsdorf and had our passports checked by the efficient, polite Austrian border police who – bless them for this! – confirmed that while the train did technically stop at Győr, due to a quirk of timetabling (or pure bloody-mindedness of the part of the Hungarian railway bureaucracy) it only came to a halt for five minutes. We needed to be ready to disembark pretty darn *schnell*. And – eyeing the mountain range of luggage blocking the hallway – it might be a really good idea to ask our fellow passengers for assistance with same.

Smiling brightly, I address the young couple and their two children sitting opposite. Won over by my admirable command of the German language – or more likely because they were friendly and obliging like all Austrians – the parents agreed to help. The children's eyes lit up at the thought of being allowed – positively encouraged! – to throw suitcases out of a train.

But first, we had to make it over the Hungarian border. It's hard to describe how powerless we felt when three tall, stern-faced young men, clad top to toe in leather (and not in an attractive way), lobbed into our carriage. Merely glancing at the passports of our new Austrian friends, they began giving us the third degree. Name, age, date of birth, reason for visiting, favourite colour? – all the while standing over us, disdain oozing from every (open) pore. Obviously, the memo about encouraging expats to return had not made it this far down the food chain. They were unfriendly, verging on hostile. Finally, having turned every page of each passport at least four times, one thug produced a stamp-pad and stamped and validated our visas. They sauntered out, ready to terrorise the occupants of the next carriage. One of them poked our luggage with his highly polished boot. "Next stop Győr!" he smirked to his buddies and they all burst out laughing.

The train entered Hungary. Watching the frozen vista flash past, my mother pressed her face to the window. As if amazed at her own bravery, she whispered, "Your father and I walked all this way…"

But there was no time for reminiscing. The helpful Austrian guard popped in to announce we had to get ready to disembark. A mad rush to grab everything, including my brother who by now was completely jetlagged and totally out of his comfort zone. As the train pulled into the station, the three of us practically fell down the steps clutching whatever we could carry. My mother was engulfed by a crowd of sobbing relatives. My brother somehow got wedged between two large ladies who I could only assume were related to us in some obscure way. I watched the rest of our belongings hurled after us, accompanied by waving and shouts of, "*Vielen Gluck! Auf Weidersein!*" The doors closed, and the train whistled past.

Some semblance of order restored, a few minutes later we made our way outside to the street where not one but two of the three taxis then currently operating in Győr were waiting to transport us to my uncle's home.

Exhausted and disoriented, I stepped into the damp of a Hungarian winter afternoon. Cold air and a light mist swirled overhead. But what struck me most was the smell – coal fires, unleaded fuel, the evocative smell of train engines. And from somewhere deep inside, a genetic memory stirred.

The weeks passed in a blur. Before landing on these frosty shores I thought myself bi-lingual. But I quickly realised that the Hungarian I spoke with my parents bore little resemblance to the machinegun rapid, shout-y speech all around me. I had been taught text book Hungarian, only to discover that the text book was well and truly out of print. Had been for quite a long time and most likely now rested in landfill.

Even my mother found it hard to catch up. Not only was our vocabulary firmly rooted in the 1950s, our pronunciation was as well. Like the country itself, the language had changed dramatically in the past two decades. And some of the changes were hilarious. Like his predecessors in the 1970s, Soviet Thug in Chief Leonid Brezhnev made no bones about the fact that the USSR considered the U S of A the source of all that was evil, depraved and dangerous. It was therefore only to be expected that Hungarians – living in this Soviet satellite completely against their will – considered that decadent country the repository of all things desirable.

Although there was a flourishing black market in Levi jeans, Marlboro cigarettes, Coca Cola and Nike runners, only Party Members could afford these luxuries. For most citizens of this egalitarian regime, this Workers' Paradise, this little piece of Socialist Nirvana, such things remained totally unattainable. But American slang? Well, that was there for the taking. Or should I say, for the talking.

The melodic, ancient language of Petőfi, Márai and Ady became littered with Americanisms. Spoken with Hungarian flare. By which I mean totally inside out and upside down. So instead of greeting someone – as we had been taught to do – with, *"jó napot kivánok"* which literally translated means, "I wish you good day" (no wonder people rolled about on the floor laughing!) the common greeting was, "See ya."

And upon departing, *"jo astet kivanok"* – I wish you good evening – was replaced with, "Hello." Yup – trendy young Hungarians now said, "See you," when they arrived and, "Hello," when they left. My little brother, busy mastering as many swear words as possible in the four short weeks allotted to him, had found willing teachers among the young sons of my uncle's friends and my mother was fighting her own battle trying to water down her posh accent. So that left only me to explain that everyone was actually saying hello when they meant goodbye and goodbye as they walked into the house. Understandably, sounding like someone who had just dropped out of an 18th century melodrama, my linguistic suggestions went unheeded.

Soon, we were seeya-ing and hello-ing with the rest.

If we found speaking to people tricky, eating everything put in front of us was even more challenging. The quality was unfailingly superb. It was the quantity that proved our undoing. We spent much of our time visiting my mother's old friends and distant relatives and this – without exception – involved consuming food. Lots and lots of food. It didn't make the blindest bit of difference what time we turned up. We were hugged, kissed, see ya'd, then made to sit down to a wonderful home cooked meal morning, noon, night and many, many times in between. Or at the very least, amid streams of apologies for not having had time to do more, we were escorted to a table groaning under cakes, biscuits and savoury pastries.

On the first few occasions we tried to explain that we had just come from a huge breakfast/lunch/dinner only to be told that the lady of the house had bribed her second cousin's son's neighbour to acquire this plump, succulent chicken. Or that the magnificent piece of roast pork displayed before us had necessitate four trips to the butcher with a bottle of red wine each time thrown in as down payment. Put like that, it would have been churlish to refuse. So, we ate. And ate. And ate.

It took me a while to work out how these lovely people could afford all this food. In the 1970s, commodities like new refrigerators, appliances and even new clothes were in short supply – the only thing readily affordable was food and drink. Most people therefore developed a, 'what the heck, we won't live long enough be able to save up for that new Westinghouse anyway' mindset and spent their earnings on what they could put into their mouths. The results were absolutely delicious. And a nightmare health-wise.

At that time, the majority of Hungarian men and women were overweight and unhealthy – due to a diet replete in carbs, sugar, red meat, all cooked in chicken, duck or goose fat. My mother – who had not been svelte since the hard days of the 1950s – looked positively slim and girlish compared to her former school friends. Type-2 diabetes was at epidemic proportions. Heart disease carried people off in their 50s and 60s.

Even the language accommodated this 'Let's all get fat together' trend. My mother and I quickly worked out that someone described as *jol nes ki* – looking good – meant overweight. While *nagyon jol nes ki* – looking very good- indicated morbid obesity. At that time, I weighed in at around 52kg (oh happy days!) and my poor mother was regularly asked why she didn't seek medical advice for my anorexic state. On one occasion, I was assured by a sweet old lady that all I needed to do to find a husband was to gain 15 kilos as soon as possible because men don't like scrawny women. Her worried expression indicated that at almost 17 years of age, I was in real danger of leaving my run a tad late.

Then Christmas arrived. And we realised that the food-fest of the previous two weeks had been no more than the warm up to the main event. Serious face-stuffing was now on the agenda.

We spent 23 December out in the country staying with my maternal grandmother. This gentle, shy lady still lived in the house they had been forced to move into in 1948 when the Hungarian Socialist Party took power. Having seized government from their democratically elected opponents, the Socialists continued to seize everything else in sight, including my mother's family's vineyards, their orchards, their fields, all their livestock and their family home. To the end of his life in 1968 (when like so many of his countrymen, he died of a massive heart attack in his early 60s) my grandfather had no option but to work his own land for the government. It had been swallowed up in a huge state-owned People's Farming Conglomerate, its offices located in his former family abode. His only consolation was tending his few remaining grapevines up on the mountainside. The only part of the estate left to him, due only to some fortuitous administrative error.

I can imagine how soul-destroying this must have been, but the system was ruthless and anyone who questioned it was severely fined or imprisoned. After spending a week in the local lock-up for insulting the authorities, my feisty, hot-headed grandfather decided to keep his opinions to himself. Hungarian is a very complex language and the words he used can't be translated accurately, but I think 'whore-loving' 'thieving' and 'bloodsucking bastards' come fairly close.

In the end, it was my little grandmother – almost as round as she was tall – who successfully took up arms against the regime. In the 1960s to the delight of her neighbours, this most reticent of women attacked the People's Farming Conglomerate Deputy. Unannounced and uninvited, he lobbed up on her doorstep one fine day to award her a medal for Good Communist Citizenship – in this case exemplified by her diligent ongoing care of the rose garden that marked the entrance to People's Farming Conglomerate Headquarters. The Commissioner of the Conglomerate had noted she regularly pruned, weeded and watered this delightful piece of communal property, for which admirable public service she was to receive a written commendation and a small silver medal.

When the medal-presenting Deputy began to apprise her of the honour now being bestowed, she was not impressed. Once part of their family lands, that rose garden had been planted by her mother-in-law and as far as she was concerned, was still very much a part of their heritage. It needed looking after and someone had to do it. Ignoring her traitorous attitude, the Deputy tried again to impress upon her the great honour being bestowed. So, she hit him. On the head. With her broom. And then chased him from the house.

The Deputy's arrival had been noticed by the neighbours. As was his hasty departure, which was celebrated with much cheering and laughing. Luckily there were no official repercussions to this anti-Soviet behaviour but from then on, my grandmother retained a 'don't mess with me' reputation in the village.

Having heard the story, my little brother was most impressed when we visited her for the first time. He asked to see the broom. A broom was produced and for the rest of our stay, John's favourite game involved yelling and running about waving it. Once or twice, he managed to persuade my grandmother to join him, thus giving her the opportunity of reliving her moment of glory as she scooted around the kitchen, remarkably nimble for her age.

But like any self-respecting Hungarian woman, most of the time she cooked.

Christmas Eve arrived, and the temperature hovered around -3. It was too cold to go out but not cold enough for snow "Just how cold does it need to get, for pity's sake?" I remember wondering and a large proportion of our time was spent – yes, you guessed correctly – eating. The house was compact – a large sitting room, which at night converted into a bedroom for my grandmother, a bedroom and kitchen, large pantry and bathroom.

My mother, John and I slept in the bedroom where my mother and I shared the enormously high double bed and John slept on a small trundle. In summer, this room would have been delightful – a high vaulted ceiling and large windows looking out onto the garden and the forest beyond. But in December, it was an icehouse. In the morning, the window was covered with frost. On the inside. Once in bed however, rugged up in our warmest PJs (which prompted the joke – "Time to get dressed and go to bed!") covered by not one but two goose-down doonas, we were toasty warm. The only danger we faced was suffocation under the weight of what felt like several dozen geese. Not only were the doonas made from hand-plucked down, the geese themselves had been raised by my grandmother. I couldn't help wondering if by some oversight a goose or three had been left intact among the feathers.

The sitting room was heated by a large green ceramic stove in the corner that would not have looked out of place in a Tolstoy novel, an observation I took care to keep to myself in this Russian-loathing climate. Sitting in a comfy chair next to the stove, munching on cake, biscuits or freshly baked rolls, I listened while my mother and grandmother reminisced. I wish with every ounce of my being that I had written down their stories. And asked all those questions that will now forever remain unanswered.

My uncle – four years younger than my mother – had married long after my parents left Hungary. Christmas Day was designated as Meet and Greet for that side of the family. My uncle didn't own a car at that point, nor did any of his close friends but my father's best friend, who had done very well for himself and was now Director of Győr's Town Planning Department, did. He kindly lent us his flashy company limousine plus driver. Why someone in this egalitarian paradise would possess such capitalist trappings was a question I was itching to ask but before I could open my mouth, my mother fixed me with a death-stare. I suspect she was wondering the same thing.

Well-fortified with an enormous breakfast, we were driven off to morning tea with my aunt's older sister's family. They lived only a few kilometres away so the enthusiastic greeting, "Come in, you must be exhausted from the trip!" was a bit over the top. As was the gourmet spread that awaited us. We tucked in bravely, consuming cakes, biscuits and fruit slices, all washed down by jet black, coronary-inducing coffee.

Abuzz with caffeine and the Hungarian equivalent of Coca Cola for my brother (called Cola Cola to clearly distinguish it from that evil western drink!) we piled into the car again to go to lunch at my aunt's brother's home. A touch of family rivalry may have been at play here – his wife produced a feast. Several different types of roast or fried meat, chicken, pheasant and fish, roast potatoes, rice with field mushrooms and many varieties of salad. Followed by cakes and puddings for dessert, including a magnificent three-layer Black Forest Cake. Covered in thick chocolate icing, oozing brandy-infused cherries and whipped cream, it tasted every bit as wonderful as it looked. I watched my brother gulp down slice after creamy slice and hoped this would not end badly.

As well as the food, there was plenty to wash it down with, including the ubiquitous *pálinka*. This national spirit was Hungary's answer to vodka. It is every bit as lethal, although if you were to question a Hungarian, they would no doubt patriotically assure you, "It's much more lethal!" Clear in colour, distilled from cherries or pears or plums – it was considered essential to get you through the cold winters. And the hot summers. As I child I remember asking my paternal grandfather – a man who liked a drink – what it tasted like. His reply, "Like a fist in the face!" was suitably off-putting. It is extremely high in alcohol – up to twice that of whisky – and regular drinkers risked permanent liver damage. Every autumn (traditional illegal *pálinka* making season) there were horror stories on national radio about entire apartment blocks collapsing when a faulty illegal distilling device exploded. Really, what's not to like?

As well as this deadly brew, there were several bottles of wine on the table. Our host proudly explained that he grew his own grapes, had been saving this particular vintage for a special occasion and was keen for our feedback. Not wanting to insult the dear man, we drank, praised, drank and then ate some more to soak up the alcohol.

Some hours later, we waddled out to be driven to the home of my aunt's younger sister. As I had seen the driver consume at least three large nips of *pálinka*, our safe arrival was by no means assured. By this stage, I was too far gone to care. But despite the alcohol gushing through his body – or as a *pálinka* connoisseur might explain – because of it! – we made it safely to our next destination. Or more accurately, to our next meal. Again, we ate and drank our body-weight although I must confess, I don't remember the details. I suspect consuming over 15,000 calories in the space of 8 hours may have contributed to memory-loss.

We finally arrived back at my grandmother's place, wanting, needing to assume the horizontal position or risk serious illness. Rolling inside, we were greeted by the smell of roasting chicken and the words, "You poor things! On the road all day! You must be starving so I've made you a nice big dinner!"

Sometime later, we lay in our bedroom spreadeagled under the geese. I really thought I was going to explode while even my mother had admitted defeat. As we fought nausea and suffocation in equal measure, a voice emerged from the direction of my brother's round little body. "This was the BEST day ever!"

Just how cold does it have to get before it snows?

CHAPTER 10
Liar, Liar. Your Regime Is On Fire!

My grandfather was a stickler for truth. He never lied, even when a little white untruth may have been more politic. We all knew not to ask his opinion on haircuts, a cleverly adapted recipe or new clothes unless we really did want to know whether, "My bottom looks big in this?"

My grandfather adored me. The only time I ever recall him being angry with me was when he caught me out in a lie. It related to a box of chocolates and a hard centre with tiny tooth marks in it, surreptitiously replaced during the hunt for my favourite strawberry cream. Having denied all knowledge of same, I was confronted by my grandfather – usually the teller of stories and giver of treats – towering over me. His blue eyes flashing, he proclaimed, not loudly but with great emphasis, "Lying is just the beginning. Someone who lies will then go on to steal. Someone who steals will then go on to commit murder." Greatly chastened, I burst into tears and apologized and for a long time remained concerned that through that one misdeed, a life of escalating crime yawned like a chasm before me.

It is a tragedy that this respect for truth was not shared by the government of the Soviet Union. A regime that not only endorsed lying but was actively underpinned by it. And just as 'a house built on sand will not stand, and its fall will be great' so eventually any system built on the distortion of the truth will come crashing down. But before it does, it inflicts untold misery.

Nowhere is this better illustrated than the fate of Hungary during and after World War II. When the Russians marched into Hungary in 1944, Stalin lied. When the troops stayed on after the war finally ended, Stalin kept lying. And the regime that was enforced on the long-suffering Hungarians after their brave but futile revolution in 1956 was possibly the biggest lie of all, although this time the porkies were told by Khrushchev, the USSR's new Fibber in Chief. My grandfather was absolutely correct – having lied, the Soviets went on to steal anything they could lay their hands on and murder countless Hungarians.

History itself became elastic, moulded to suit whoever was writing it. According to the Soviet version, Hungary was 'liberated' rather than conquered by the brave Red Army during the desperate Siege of Budapest, which lasted from December 1944 until February 1945. Over 50,000 Hungarian soldiers and 38,000 civilians perished as the gracious houses and mansions of Buda were reduced to rubble. The majestic bridges – once the pride of Europe – that connected the twin towns were blown up. Old men, women and children succumbed to starvation or typhoid from drinking contaminated water. Conditions were no better on the Pest side. Hand to hand combat in the narrow alleyways, entire apartment blocks ripped apart by tanks. Skeletons of dead horses littering the streets, hacked to pieces by starving inhabitants.

But when the Nazis and Hungarian Arrow Cross troops were finally defeated by the Red Army in early 1945, the Russian liberators began their own reign of terror. An estimated 40,000 young girls and women were raped and many more murdered. Anyone suspected of having supported the Nazi regime was packed off to Russian labour camps. Some 10,000 families were thrown out of their homes and shipped to remote villages. Their only crime – being middle class. These newly denounced Enemies of the People were put to work on the land. Doctors, lawyers, journalists all toiled from morning until night in terrible conditions digging, planting, harvesting. Wasting their expertise and experience when the country needed them more than ever. Meanwhile, Russian officers and their families moved into their houses and the Party faithful took over their jobs. The economic collapse that resulted was as dire as it was inevitable.

Each lie built on the one before. Just as Hungary had asked the USSR to come to her aid in 1944, Hungary went on to 'request Soviet assistance' to recover from the destruction of the war years. Then Hungary 'needed her Soviet brothers' to help her prepare for democratic elections. And my personal favourite distortion of the truth? Even though the Soviet supported and controlled Hungarian Socialist Party won only 17% of the votes in 1948, the Hungarian people were asking, positively begging! for a socialist government. And so that is what they got. A government that was Soviet bred, Soviet fed, Soviet led.

Lies spread like a virus, permeating Hungarian society and infecting the very fabric of everyday life. An entire social system built on the rejection of honesty and fear of the truth.

In 1848 Marx described the perfect society, an egalitarian nirvana, which would be underpinned by a single principle:

'From each according to his ability, to each according to his needs'.

Closely observing how this played out for the common people during my frequent trips back to Hungary in the late 1970s and 1980s, all I can say is – obviously the Hungarian Socialist Workers' Party had not read Marx.

Not only was inequality and corruption embedded in Hungarian society, after a while it defined it, held in place by exaggeration, deception and propaganda. Take the health system for example. 'The finest quality health care is free and readily available to all citizens!' the government proudly proclaimed. Except much of the time, it was not readily available. And at no time was it free.

The only way you could get to a doctor worthy of the name was to bribe the many people who stood between you and this particular servant of the people. The man who managed the medical centre. The woman who scheduled the appointments. The women who opened the door for you and took down your medical history. The woman who handed you the specimen jar and pointed the way to the toilet. Each and every person had to be given money before you finally got to go from the dingy, cold waiting room to the even dingier, freezing surgery and stripped down to your undies in front of the doctor. Of course, it then went without saying that he or she had to be given the largest sweetener of all if you were to have any hope of recovery. And please, don't get me started on how convoluted and expensive it was to obtain quality pharmaceuticals!

I don't blame the individual participants in this farce. They were stuck in a rotten system. Criminally underpaid and expected to supplement their earnings in this way. They weren't accepting – or more accurately, demanding – tips to fuel their collective drug habit. They needed the extra cash to be able to afford luxuries like food and rent. Money under the table underpinned the system. The dirty little secret everyone knew, everyone participated in, but no-one spoke about. If, as the government claimed, Hungary's healthcare system was indeed the most efficient and effective of the Eastern Bloc, God help those poor wretches in the other countries!

It was the same everywhere. I totally understood the tipping etiquette for hospitality workers, hairdressers, taxi drivers and the like, but slipping money to the man who came to read your gas meter? The woman who delivered the mail? Really?

The whole 'according to his needs' equality myth took another sharp smack in the head when you went shopping. Every major Hungarian city had Dollar Shops. Unlike their much later namesakes, these did not sell cute nick-knacks you didn't know you needed but bought anyway for a few dollars. No – these Dollar Shops sold Luxury Items – the best quality food, fine soap, exclusive cosmetics, furs, premium wine and spirits, Herend porcelain, intricately embroidered handicrafts, cashmere jumpers and shawls, caviar, pate, Russian champagne. All those things not available in the uniformly drab, unappealing shops frequented by the general population. The Dollar Shops got their name because to shop in one, you either had to use foreign currency – or more to the point American Dollars – or rank among the highest echelons of the Hungarian Communist Party. Equality? Not so much.

In those far off days, the Australia dollar compared very favourably with the US dollar so once I converted my holiday spending money into US currency, I felt very wealthy. And no matter how much I disapproved in principle, without doubt shopping in the Dollar Shops was a lovely experience. No lingering scent of boiled cabbage and stale salami. No sticky floors that made your footsteps echo like slaps. No rude shop assistants. Instead, upon entering you were immersed in soft lighting, gentle music and the faintest whiff of French perfume to get you in the mood. Uncrowded, unstressed. And for everyone except tourists and the elite few – unattainable.

But the best bit as far as I was concerned was how simple it was to actually buy something in these shops. You went inside, selected what you wanted, parted with your filthy immoral western lucre and received the beautifully wrapped parcel in one smooth, effortless transaction. You were even offered a pretty paper bag to hold your purchase from the salesgirl who smiled while bidding you a friendly goodbye on your way out. Sometimes she even opened the door for you!

It was a million light years away from the nightmare of Triple Queuing, a weird ritual that helped guarantee full employment and frayed nerves. This quaint feature of the socialist shopping experience really did my head in. Let's imagine you need to buy bread. First you enter the bakery and say, *"jó reggelt"* – wishing everyone Good Morning. No-one responds, although a few elderly shoppers may smile at you before looking away quickly when they remember this is no longer acceptable behaviour. The surly shop assistants certainly never acknowledge your greeting. Why would they? They are selling what you need, and, with all jobs guaranteed by the government and promotion based on having the right contacts, a fixed stare will do just as well as a pleasant hello.

The unilateral exchange of greeting complete, you begin to Queue. Or should I say Queues.

Queue No 1. Placed furthest away from the door, this queue allows you to stand behind a whole heap of people and slowly make your way to the front counter, positioned at such a height and angle that you can't see what is displayed until you are pressed right up against it. Once in position, trying to ignore the heavy breath of the person behind you, you examine the offerings – crusty loaves, small crisp rolls, tangy black bread, the whole deliciously fragrant selection. Having inhaled the scent of the bread for a brief moment, you tell the shop assistant scowling at you from behind the counter what you wish to purchase. She doesn't so much as blink to confirm she understands your order. She scrawls something on the scrap of paper she then hands you. Her writing is totally illegible so, living in the hope that you actually get what you asked for, you

Move to Your Left to Join the Next Queue.

Queue No 2. This one proceeds more quickly but does not reward you with a pleasant olfactory experience when you reach the front. Instead, you are eye-balled by another surly shop assistant. You hand her the paper with the hieroglyphics and she tells you how much your purchase costs. You pay her. She hands you another bit of paper – the receipt. And then you

Move to Your Left to Join the Next Queue.

Queue No 3. usually moves the fastest. Which is just as well because by this time, although the shop is a five-minute walk from your house, you have been away for the best part of an hour and your family is beginning to worry.

This last queue is the Business End of the transaction. Here, in return for your receipt, another dour saleslady (obviously related to the other two) hands you your purchase. Or what you hope is your purchase because if some misstep has occurred during the elaborate barn-dance that passes for shopping in this part of world and you end up with someone else's order, back you go to Queue No 1.

No argument. No exemptions. No mercy. No bread.

Assuming you get the bread rolls you set off so very long ago to buy for breakfast and hopefully will now get home in time for lunch, you put them into the string or hessian bag you brought with you. Plastic or paper bags are not given out in shops. If you forget to bring a bag (as I usually did), you carry the bread home in your bare hands.

Number of queues – three. Number of shop assistants – three. Number of hours wasted – countless. But as the government liked to boast, "There is no unemployment in Hungary!" And if there ever was, all they needed to do was insert another queue. Instant 25% job-growth. Simple.

But things could have been worse, or so I discovered on my first solo bread shopping expedition. It had not occurred to me to ask for a protocol briefing before leaving home and I got it totally wrong. I wished everyone a cheery Good Morning upon entering and then went STRAIGHT TO QUEUE NO 3!

Shocked into silence, not a single customer said anything to indicate I had broken all the rules. When I got to the head of the line, the saleswomen asked for my receipt. As it was obvious to everyone except me that I had not participated in the Queue 1 and 2 experiences, this was very unkind. When I stammered that I didn't have a receipt, and may I please have six bread-rolls and a rye loaf, she just glared at me before pointing to Queue No 1, ordering me to, "Start there!"

She didn't add, "You moronic, spoilt, imbecilic Capitalist oppressor of the working-class!" but that was clearly implied. Greatly chastened, I did as I was told and finally emerged with my purchases. It was the most humiliating experience of my – admittedly sheltered – life and I never made that mistake again.

On returning home, I told my aunt what had happened. She was very sympathetic but then put the whole fraught experience into perspective.

"At least now we have bread!" she said. Oh.

One of the most inexplicable things to me among the many inexplicable things – was how unfriendly people were when they were serving you. Queuing next to you. Stabbing you with their baguette on the bus. Pushing past you on the street. Silent. Morose. Hostile.

It didn't make sense. All the people we met socially – everyone from my aunt's mother's next-door neighbour to the lady who had lived across the street from my grandparents 30 years earlier, to say nothing of all our relatives and friends – were delightful. They could not have been more friendly, welcoming, hospitable, generous. Everyone showered us with food, love, hugs, wine, flowers, chocolates, more food. It took me a while to realize that to survive here, most people developed multiple personality disorder. They had a private persona – their friendly, generous side, which they revealed to family and friends but kept carefully hidden during working hours. Then there was their public persona – cold, often downright unpleasant – model citizens of this Workers' Paradise, loyal to the socialist ideal. What a soul-destroying, dishonest way to live!

Another great communist lie was that every innovation, every new way of doing things was initiated 'due to public demand'. Housing was a good example. In the late 1960s, the powers-that-be in the Hungarian People's Socialist Republic were faced with an acute housing shortage for the many families who were moving from small country towns into the cities, where all the jobs were. They needed to provide accommodation for hundreds of thousands of people as quickly (and cheaply) as possible. Following the Russian example, the government decided that large-scale development of apartment blocks was the way to go. This meant the destruction of entire neighbourhoods, which even in this totalitarian society, was unlikely to go down well. So, to justify all the free-standing houses that had to be demolished, the Hungarian Socialist Department of Planning and Housing published the results of a survey.

According to the press, this National Questionnaire was completed by over 85% of the adult population. And to the delight of the government, it revealed that 89% of respondents believed it was 'far healthier and more desirable' to live in apartments than in houses. So that is what the government was going to build for them. Job done! Sounds fair enough. Except not only did I never meet anyone who had participated in this survey, I never even met anyone who knew anyone who had.

It was all a big fat fabrication, which was intended to result in a big fat prefabrication. In my home town Győr, as all around the country, they demolished street after street of attractive detached houses, bulldozing their orchards and gardens to create a mini-city of multi-story apartments of incredible uniform ugliness. Every single building component – walls, windows, doors, roof, drain-pipes, floorboards – was manufactured in Russia and transported partly assembled to Hungary. Believed me, it showed.

On our first two trips back, my mother's brother, his wife and young daughter lived in one of these, 'Made in Russia Monstrosities', so we got to fully immerse ourselves in the much-lauded Social Housing Improvement Program when we stayed with them.

Their apartment was on the third floor. The building was one of five identical four-story eyesores. A narrow strip of broken concrete separated each building. Every apartment had a tiny balcony, on which one person at a time could stand to admire the garbage dumpsters attractively arranged out the front. These overflowed regularly, further enhancing the scene with a decoupage of litter. Pre-1948, the street was called *Alma Utca* (Apple Street), testimony to the large gardens with fruit trees behind every house. Now renamed *Ipar Utca* (Industrial Street), its name accurately summed up the transformation.

The building's original sparkling white exterior quickly faded to the pale grey of a three-day-old cadaver. The entry foyer was tiled in tiny flesh-coloured tiles that extended all the way up the staircase and along each corridor. Going in and up felt like being swallowed and propelled along an oesophagus, to be spit out onto the landing. The staircase was steep, dark and dangerous – the building project had not only been delivered faster than scheduled but also below budget, obviously with significant savings on tile glue. Within six months of completion, the foyer tiles were popping off almost daily, the front door frames were warped and the windows either didn't open or couldn't be closed. In a typical Hungarian winter, the latter was more than mild inconvenience.

Once you managed to get upstairs without breaking a leg on the uneven stairs or being cut by the knife-like edge of a falling tile, the apartments themselves were remarkably light and comfortable, albeit cozy. A small bedroom, a large '*napali*' (day room), compact kitchen and tiny bathroom, most of which was taken up by the enormous gas hot water heater. Also manufactured in and imported from the USSR, this potentially lethal appliance featured the company logo – a jolly cartoon lion – proudly displayed on the front. Given the number of lethal explosions that resulted every year from leaking gas, it should have featured a Skull and Crossbones.

Some of the families living in my uncle's building had been given their apartments to compensate for having their houses requisitioned, thus adding insult to injury. But everyone seemed to make the best of it and there was a real sense of community in each building.

Most couples had only one child and even then, it would have been a tight fit. But many also had one, sometimes two, grandparents living with them. But Hungarians are nothing if not inventive. They rose to the challenge and by the early 1970s, an entire industry had evolved designing and manufacturing incredibly clever, stylish multi-purpose furniture, thus allowing these tiny apartments to comfortable accommodate three or four adults and a child or two.

Usually the parents slept on a sofa bed, but dining tables could also be converted into double beds by a clever winding mechanism that lowered it to the requisite height, topped by an air mattress. Even dining chairs were designed to extend and slot together with their backs folded down to create a single bed. One Christmas when our entire family visited, while my aunt and uncle slept on their sofa bed in the *napali* as usual, my parents slept on the converted dining table in the same room and my brother and I each had a single bed/dining chair conversion, joining my cousin in her tiny bedroom. Wall to wall people it might have been, but we were all very comfortable and had a wonderful six weeks holiday.

Every day, every Hungarian was forced to pay lip service to the lies invented by the regime. And on one occasion, so was I. I had just completed my law degree and fearing that long overseas vacations would be but a memory once I began my new life as an overworked, underpaid newly qualified solicitor at the very bottom of the food chain of the firm that had just hired me, I managed to delay my start date until August. This gave me six glorious weeks in which to enjoy the delights of the European summer, including in Hungary.

Before flying out, my mother told me that she intended to buy my uncle a car while I was staying with them. Or rather, she was giving me money that I would then use to buy him the car. It all sounded fairly simple and I raised no objection. I thought it was a lovely, generous thing for her to do and I planned to add my own gift of car-seat covers and a pair of furry dice to hang in the front window of the new vehicle.

Of course, being Socialist Hungary, it turned out to be anything but simple, as my mother well knew when she handed me the assignment. She decided, correctly as it turned out, that having agreed to do it, I was unlikely to back out when the full details were disclosed to me upon arrival. I was very fond of my uncle and his family and their fate, or should I say their car, was in my hands.

The transaction was so complicated, to say nothing of bizarre, that my uncle had to explain it to me several times before I understood what was required of me. It turned out that buying a brand-new car in Hungary was impossible unless you were a member of the political elite – only they could afford or had access to this luxury. But, and it was a very Big But, if you had a relative from overseas who was willing to play along, you could participate in an elaborate charade (more accurately – a big fat lie) whereby you eventually ended up with a car and the government got lots of lovely $US. All because your relative agreed to commit perjury.

Basically, I had to pretend I was buying the car for myself, using my own foreign currency. It made a lot of sense – I mean why wouldn't I buy a car in Hungary when I live in Australia? But this was how everyone was doing it. The government knew all about it and had actually set up the system under which a tourist could – after one month after taking possession of said vehicle – transfer ownership of the car to a Hungarian citizen. For which you paid another fee, naturally.

The paperwork was horrendous – pages and pages of declarations and forms. Once these had been lodged and returned, which took about two weeks, the purchaser (me) had to meet with someone from the Department of Automotive Sales. This is the best translation I can come up with although a more accurate name would be Department of Automotive Deceit. The Department was in Budapest so my uncle, aunt, cousin and I travelled down by train. We had a lovely morning sightseeing, eating ice-cream and generally enjoying ourselves until noon when my cousin and aunt went across the river to see the Palace Museum in Buda. I headed off accompanied by my uncle to complete the transaction.

The total purchase price had already been paid and so all that was left was the interview, after which I would be the proud owner of a brand-new white Trabant. This really was stretching credibility waaay too far. If I was going to buy a car overseas, wouldn't it be a smart Porsche or a classy BMW? Or my very favourite at that time – a snappy little MG? But Trabants were the only car then available in Hungary. Unless you were in government, in which case, you were given a Zhiguli, that ubiquitous Soviet car beloved of Politburochiefs. And gangsters. Which usually was one and the same person.

When my little brother first saw a Trabant, he declared, "That's not a car!" Everyone outside the Soviet Bloc agreed but to most Hungarians in the early 1980s, it represented their greatest aspiration. Produced between 1957 and 1990, East German designed and manufactured, the Trabant – or Traubie as Hungarians affectionately called it – eventually became a symbol of all that was wrong with the Eastern Bloc. When the Berlin Wall came down in 1989, elated East Germans abandoned their Trabants by the thousands on the border as they made their way to West Germany and superior vehicular design.

Squat and square in shape, the Trabant was a small, noisy, smelly, exhaust-belching box on wheels. The exterior was made of something similar to pressed cardboard coated in a waterproof substance. Two Trabants running into each other was not much of a problem – the 500cc two-cylinder two-stroke engine ensured speed did not kill. But many fatalities occurred when the poor little box ended up under a truck. Or collided with a foreign-made car. Or, as happened regularly in the countryside, a herd of cows.

By the time I set my heart on buying my very own little Traubie, the most popular model was the Trabant 601. Still square, still ugly, still noisy, it now offered unheard of luxuries like interior lighting and back windscreen wipers. I could hardly wait.

But wait I did for about 90 minutes in the reception room before my uncle and I were ushered into the office to meet the official and complete the purchase. My uncle was becoming increasingly nervous. I'm not sure if it was because at that time, Hungarians usually became nervous when faced with officialdom. With good reason, I may add. Or if he was worried that I would refuse to continue the charade. Although I had agreed to play this silly game, I had let him know in no uncertain terms what a farce I thought it all was. My disapproval was almost palpable, and I suspect my uncle was praying I would refrain from sharing my thoughts at this critical point in the proceedings.

The official was a large man sitting behind a large desk on an enormous chair, which was clearly hoping to be a throne when it grew up. The man was clearly hoping to be promoted to head of department when he grew up so took his job very seriously. Shaking my hand, he made small talk for a few minutes, asking where I came from. This must have been part of the script because he had my passport, my Hungarian Visa and many pages of Car Purchase Application Form in front of him.

When he heard I was from Sydney, he beamed. "You might know my cousin? He lives in Melbourne." I could feel my uncle tense. Instead of a short sharp geography lesson, I smiled back and agreed that yes, I might.

After a few more inane comments, we got down to business. He went through the great wad of documents and then asked the big question. My uncle had prepped me for this and I was ready.

"So," said my new friend with the Melbourne-dwelling relative, "You want to buy a Trabant." It was not so much a question as a declaration of intent.

"Look, can we please stop insulting each other's intelligence? We both know I have no intention of buying this lame excuse for automotive engineering. Why would I? It's a pile of junk and not even attractive junk. Anyway, how the hell am I supposed to get it home to Sydney when I leave next month? As hand luggage maybe?

"So, no. I do not want to buy this badly designed semi-waterproof cardboard box on wheels.

"But I DO want my uncle to achieve his great desire. He is a good, honest person who has had a very hard life and if owning a car, even one like this, gives him some modicum of happiness, I'm prepare to endanger my soul to eternal damnation by lying!"

Of course, I didn't say that. I smiled politely and said, "Yes, thank you. I want to buy a Trabant." My uncle stopped holding his breath.

And that did the trick. After asking me to sign yet another form, the man handed back my passport and Visa and walked us to the door.

"Congratulations," he shook my hand.

Out on the street, my uncle hugged me. "Thank you!" he said. I almost burst into tears. The joy-zapping inhumanity of this regime was enough to break anyone. Yet here he was, this dear man, thanking me for helping him achieve his dream by lying through my clenched teeth.

"When will the car be delivered? Or do I have to go and pick it up?" I asked.

"They will telephone me when its ready to be collected. In about six months I think!"

Although the full purchase price of the car had to be paid when the Application Form was lodged, the car would not be available for many months? Are you kidding me?

No. Apparently, this is how it was done.

"But won't I have to collect it myself? Do I have to come back in January to take delivery?" I was already wondering how to ask my new employer for another week off. To take delivery of my new car. In Hungary.

"Oh no," my uncle reassured me. "All you need to do is sign another form. That will allow me to take delivery of it for you. And a month later, I can transfer it into my own name."

I was speechless. What a total waste of time and effort! What a great big fat lie!

But there was nothing I could do – this was the system they lived under. And my uncle looked totally elated.

"OK," I said. "Let's go meet the others. And then, I'm taking everyone out for a special lunch to celebrate. But first, is there anywhere in Budapest where I can buy a pair of furry dice?"

With my cousin in Budapest, before heading off to commit perjury to buy my very own little 'Traubi'.

CHAPTER 11
The Diggers' Club

"Scratch a Hungarian, find soil."

According to my mother, an old saying and I think it's fairly accurate, although some nuance may be lost in the translation. There is no doubt that most Hungarians are immersed in their love of the soil. Gerald O'Hara's declaration in *Gone with the Wind*, "It's the land, Katie Scarlett! The land! The only thing worth fighting for. Worth dying for!" would have resonated with my ancestors.

Hungary was an agricultural country from ancient times. From the rich red soil of the eastern part down to the loamier less fertile western plain, the people grew crops – wheat, maize, corn and barley – and grazed vast herds of cattle and sheep. From around the 1800s, vineyards were added and in the nineteenth and early twentieth centuries, Hungarian white and red wine was justly famous. Tsar Alexander II of Russia is reputed to have loved *Tokaj Aszú*, christening this delicious pale golden dessert tipple, 'Wine of Kings, King of Wines'. Then there was the famous *Egri Bikavér* – Bull's Blood of Eger – deep crimson, high alcohol content, a blend of several grape varieties, aged for many years in oak. Reputedly it was one of several go-to beverages for Napoleon Bonaparte, who was introduced to it in 1809.

It may have helped him drown his sorrows after the Austrians wiped the floor with his Italian allies in the Battle of Raab.

Before World War I killed off the dream that was Continental Europe, over 70% of Hungary was devoted to agriculture. Three percent of the landowning population were very rich and 38% were very poor. Five immensely wealthy families – Esterházy, Apponyi, Festetics, Báthory and Batthyány – possessed almost a third of the land. A further 5,000 families owned another 37% of the land, while most of the rest was owned by 66,000 middle-class families. The meagre remnants belonged to the peasants, including 1000 wealthier peasant families who had around 30 hectares each. The rest – approximately 3.5 million peasants – tried to eke out a living, mostly by hiring themselves as contract labour to the big landholdings.

But even then, everyone except the poorest of the poor had their own little plot of land – where they grew potatoes, carrots, cabbages. Any spare space was filled with sunflowers, grown not just for their spectacular displays but for their delicious seeds and golden oil. And right up to the Second World War, ever the smallest vineyards grew roses; each row of vines planted foot and head with a rosebush. Experts opined this was because a good flush of roses in June heralded a good grape harvest in autumn. But I think it was far less scientific than that. Hungarians loved growing roses – the heady scented flowers with their silky petals every bit as satisfying in their own way as bunches of sweet ripe grapes.

In spring, Hungarian meadows are crimson with poppies while in summer, fields of sunflowers stretch as far as the eye can see. Even after the Soviets nationalised all land-holdings in 1948, and families suddenly found themselves employed by the state to work the land their families had owned for generations, any Hungarian who could afford it bought their own patch of dirt. City dwellers headed out to their miniscule plots on Saturday afternoon, happy to get their hands dirty and to supplement the unappetising produce in the shops with their home-grown potatoes, carrots, beans, lettuce and tomatoes. These gardens usually contained a tiny one-room cabin originally called *dachas* – the Russian word for country home. But the Hungarians hated the Russian name – let's face it, they hated Russian everything full stop. So increasingly over the years, these retreats began to be known as *weekend ház* – weekend houses. Uncle Sam winning hands down over Uncle Joe, if only in this small way.

Along with everyone else, my maternal grandfather's vineyards were subsumed into the vast local landholdings. But through a fortuitous error in one of the title deeds, he managed to keep a plot – hardly more than two acres – on top of the hill. This was a source of great family pride. Not only was it significantly larger than the plots of all the other villagers, it even had a two-room hut with a wine-cellar excavated deep below it. In the old days, enormous wine barrels took up most of the cellar, while the rooms above were used as lodgings for the itinerant labourers brought in for the harvest.

My grandfather and, after his death, my uncle carefully tended the symmetrical rows of grapevines and in autumn, pressed the grapes to make their own wine, once more putting to good use the ancient barrels in the cellar. The dried grape skins were used to make *palinka*, the lethal spirit so beloved of Hungarians. A dozen *megy* (Morello cherry) trees planted around the perimeter produced bumper crops of tart, delicious fruit and raspberry bushes and strawberry plants also featured prominently. At the height of summer, the scent of berries greeted you long before you reached the summit of the hill.

Menjünk a hegyba! Staying with my uncle's family, these were very welcome words.

"Let's go to the mountain!" he would declare and off we would go to spend a day or two immersed in nature. Located not exactly on a mountain, more like a big hill, but right on the summit, the hut was just roomy enough for three double bunk beds, a squishy old sofa, a big old pine table and six carved chairs. In the smaller room, there was a kitchen of sorts along one wall – a sink, an ice cooled camping refrigerator and a gas hotplate connected – a bit precariously even to my untrained eye – to a gas bottle. Luckily, it was rarely used. Food was cooked outside on a fire fuelled with fragrant cherry wood. Meals were eaten sitting at the table relocated under the trees.

Although we made regular pilgrimages back to Hungary after that first momentous trip, we had always gone during the Australian Christmas holidays – in the Hungarian winter. No-one in full possession of their sanity went up the mountain in winter - the snow was usually high enough to reach the roof of the cabin and the road unpassable. But finally, again accompanied by my mother and brother, I made a summer visit and experienced what was left of our once significant ancestral acres in all its verdant glory.

Before my uncle purchased his own car, he was able to borrow a car from the postal department where he worked. From the late-1970s, post office staff above a certain managerial level could apply for and be assigned a car once a month. This system was launched with great fan-fare as another illustration of vision and generosity, yet another fine example of the munificence of the regime. What no-one mentioned – or no one who actually wanted to hold onto their job, that is – was that the comrades perched on the top of the postal department tree were very bit as fat and glossy as in any capitalist regime. In many cases, they not only owned their own cars (sometimes even a Mercedes or

Vauxhall, which had now replaced the ubiquitous Szigoulis of earlier years) but had their own drivers, lived in large modern houses in town and enjoyed luxurious holiday in beautiful villas on Lake Balaton and the Bakony Mountains.

But my uncle was happy enough with a little Trabant to drive the 28km from Győr to the village of Gecse. Unable to take the whole family plus all the stuff we needed for our stay in one go, he made several trips. With me squashed into the back seat amidst numerous bags and boxes and my mother wedged into the none-too-spacious passenger seat, we set off.

At that time in my life (and let's not lie about this – ever since) I liked my little luxuries. Or more accurately, I liked my luxuries to be as large as possible. And as often as possible. Thank you. Back-packing had never appealed. Camping was not on my agenda and the only stars I longed to sleep under were five. A friend at university once commented that I thought 'roughing it' meant not having a hairdryer within reach. A tad harsh maybe, but accurate.

Conditions in Hungary had been an eye-opener but even in Győr, although our living arrangements were cosy to say the least, we had a fully functioning albeit teeny weeny bathroom, hot water and a toilet that flushed at least 90% of the time. So, staying in a mountain shack, even for three nights, was nowhere near my idea of heaven.

As my uncle drove and waxed lyrical about our upcoming mini-break, I began to fear the worst. The bedroom was lovely and cool, with windows on both sides to create a through-breeze. The kitchen was basic but more than adequate, he enthused.

"And the bathroom?" I enquired politely. Ignoring me, he went on to describe the view – vast open fields below, the mountains beyond…

"The bathroom?" I tried again.

I would love the forest walks. The pretty woodland paths surrounding the property.

"Bathroom?"

At that point, my mother intervened.

"There is running water, and an outhouse with lots of bushes for privacy. Now shut up!"

I did. But curled up on the back seat feeling seriously hard done by, I was certain I would hate it.

I was wrong. I loved it. Outhouse or no outhouse. From the moment I climbed from the car to be engulfed by the scent of summer, I adored it. I had never realised that summer had a fragrance. But it did here – of ripening strawberries, succulent raspberries, freshly scythed hay, tender new growth.

There were six of us in total. The hut slept exactly that number but because the weather was so lovely, we all decided to sleep in hammocks outside. Totally unlike my 'double innerspring mattress, thick mattress topper, linen sheets and fluffy goose-feather pillows' persona. If I had not taken photographic proof, on my return to Sydney, none of my friends would have believed me.

Strung between two tall cherry trees, my hammock was surprisingly comfortable. Mosquitoes didn't venture this far up, the air was balmy and fragrant, and I slept like a log only to be awakened at dawn by the chorus of roosters in the village below.

And there on our hill, Dawn, exquisite Dawn became my new friend. She and I – well, it would be accurate to say we had not been buddies before, although we had met a couple of times back in Australia. When I staggered home from an all-night party, Dawn occasionally made a cameo appearance and we might even hang out together for a while. But certainly not in a 'let's exchange phone numbers so we can catch up' kind of way. We were passing acquaintances and that suited me just fine.

But up here, early morning was breathtaking. Dawn in all her glory. Wrapped in a blanket, hugging a hot cup of coffee, I watched her slowly paint the black mountains scarlet, gold and finally emerald green as the dew on the grass glistened.

But my strongest memories of this time centre on food. Hot freshly baked rolls for breakfast and lunch. Just picked cherries. Raspberries and strawberries warm from the sun, exploding with flavour when you bit into them. Fresh goat's cheese purchased from our nearest neighbour. Pale golden butter, softly clinging straight out of the churn. A true Chekhovian idyll, although I took care to keep this Russian analogy to myself.

Dinners were the highlight. Having insisted on taking over the cooking from my aunt, my mother outdid herself. She baked mushrooms. Gathered from the forest that morning, big as dinner plates, she filled them with a cheese, wine, breadcrumb and herb mixture. Round red capsicums stuffed with rice, bacon, fried onion and parsley in a piquant tomato sauce. Small pieces of *salona* (pancetta) and *kolbász* (a thick spicy pork sausage) fried together with diced onion, garlic, yellow peppers and tomatoes to make *letcso*. A typical peasant meal eaten with rye bread to mop up the delicious sauce.

And my very favourite – *lángos*. Pronounced laang – osh, this is Hungarian folk-cuisine at its finest. A cross between flatbread and pizza, traditionally made using just four ingredients – flour, yeast, water and salt. The dough is left to rise, rolled out then cut into squares and deep fried in oil or pork fat. Topped with sour cream and chives, or grated cheese or just rubbed with garlic and olive oil, *lángos* made its way around Europe. The journey has not been without peril – in some countries it has morphed into a sweet offering or is made using mashed potato instead of flour. While the result may be tasty, nothing beats the original recipe.

My mother was a dab hand and regularly made *lángos* at home for a simple supper or lunch. But the best I ever recall her making was right there on that hilltop. Pillowy soft dough put out to rise in the shade of the trees, then fried in a huge skillet over the cherry-wood fire. Drizzled with pale green freshly pressed olive oil and rubbed with a garlic clove that less than an hour before had been growing in the veggie patch. All washed down with copious amounts of home-made red wine.

When I picture my mother in the ten years since she died, she is usually in her kitchen in Sydney cooking up a storm. But one of my most precious memories of her is during that summer. Encased in a big white apron, hair tied back with a red scarf, her hands covered in flour. She stands at the big table and expertly kneads *lángos*. Noticing me loitering in the doorway, she looks up, smiles and waves one of her dough covered hands. Totally herself, totally at home in this unpretentious cabin that had been in her family for decades.

Living with one foot firmly planted in Sydney, the other in her ancestral home. It was both a curse and a blessing. And one of the things that made her who she was.

Watching my uncle happily prune the grapevines, tend the berry bushes and cherry trees, he did not look to me like a man who harboured any ill-feeling against the government that had helped itself to his birthright. Like many Hungarians who ended up staying here in 1956, he seemed to have made his peace with the regime and just got on with things as best he could. I suspect resentment was a luxury he could ill afford.

On the other hand, even from the little she said about it, I'm sure my mother was furious at the government sanctioned theft – let's call it what it was. But not as furious as when she was magnanimously offered the opportunity to reclaim what they had filched.

To the amazement of most people – including its own citizens and anyone else unfortunate enough to be subjected to its repressive dictatorship – in the late 1980s, the USSR fell apart. Having murdered countless millions and oppressed many millions more, the once seemingly invincible regime sort of just… fizzled out. Deflated like an old balloon with insufficient air. More than 30 years after brave Hungarian students marched through Budapest chanting, "Ruski go home! Go! Go" they finally did. Thankfully without violence, without bloodshed. The detested Russian army quietly packed up its loathsome hammer, sickle, rifles, and warped ideology and slunk off home.

This left innumerable and at times insurmountable problems for the government. Although suddenly no longer a People's Democratic Republic, Hungary was still very far from being a democracy. It's economy, now no longer based on the socialist model, was certainly not capitalist, although wanting very much to be.

Amidst this confusion, things quickly unravelled. Inflation soared as the hapless Hungarians discovered they needed to rebuild much of their heavy industry as well as revitalise the agricultural heritage that had been trampled beneath the boot of collectivism.

To do this, the new government desperately needed money. Or to be more accurate – needed *valuta* – foreign currency. Massive amounts of it. And so, over the next few years, it devised several ingenious schemes to attract it. One of these was Historical Ownership Buyback. A morally – and probably legally – questionable scheme offering to sell back to the original owners the land it had forcibly acquired from them in the late 1940s.

I have no idea how successful this plan was overall, but my mother wasn't having a bar of it.

Calling in on my parents one summer day in 1993, I found my father pottering about in the garage, where he had taken sanctuary from my mother who was in the kitchen cooking, venting her rage by banging pots and pans. She had just received a letter – very formal and official looking – from the Hungarian government. In flowery language that I won't even attempt to translate, it cordially invited her to buy back the family's vast land holdings. It even told her the price had been significantly discounted – due to 'prior historical ownership rights'.

Sadly, my uncle died in 1992. Like too many of his countrymen, his unhealthy lifestyle carried him off aged only 54 from a fatal heart attack. My maternal grandmother was still very much alive but the government – or rather the Department of Rural Land (Historical Ownership Division?) obviously decided its best chance of milking this scheme lay not with the sweet little old lady living in the small village in rural Hungary but with her foreign dwelling (therefore presumably well-heeled) daughter.

It couldn't have been more wrong. There was no way on God's fair earth that my mother was going to play their stupid – and in her view immensely insulting – game.

I must admit I was very tempted. I loved the idea of once again owning land that had been in my family for many generations. Ancestral Soil! Mother Earth! I had a vision of returning one day, rebuilding the old manor house – demolished to make way for a road many years ago – and living in Arcadia amidst golden wheat fields and lush vineyards. I could see myself in a long white lace dress and big straw hat, woven basket over my arm, picking roses for the drawing room while hard-working, generously remunerated devoted loyal labourers tilled my fields. *Anna Karenina* meets *Under the Tuscan Sun*.

My mother may also have seen a vision of herself – as she was in November 1956. Dispossessed, cold, terrified, trudging with my father across the Austro-Hungarian border, while Russian soldiers used them for target practice. They had threatened her life. They had taken her land. Now they wanted to sell it back to her! No. No. And no!

Very wisely, my father stayed out of the debate. He emerged only momentarily from the safety of the garage to suggest it would be extremely unwise of me to try to persuade my mother to go down the Buy Back What They Stole Route. Listening to the clashing of saucepans, I reluctantly admitted he had a point. Obviously, her vision shot mine down in flames and that was that. My mother didn't think the letter merited a reply and she never heard from the government again.

Initially unable, eventually unwilling to reclaim her ancestral land, she devoted herself to every centimetre of her garden in Sydney. Their first house in Annandale – the large run-down federation villa they managed to resurrect on the smell of an oily rag – had a sizeable – and very neglected – garden. But backbreaking hard work and sheer exhaustion left them little time for gentle pursuits like gardening. Apart from pruning the old fruit trees and keeping the lawn mowed, nothing else was done to the big block.

It wasn't until they moved to their dream location – Sydney's northern beaches – that my mother finally had the opportunity to awaken her inner green thumb. There was much to do here, and she took to it with relish. The original weather-board beach house sat on a large block of land but apart from a few straggly azalea bushes, a couple of pine trees and masses of honeysuckle trying to strangle everything in its path, there was no garden to speak of. Just sandy soil, strong northerly winds, sea air.

When she told her friendly neighbour soon after moving in that she planned to establish a rose garden at the front of the house, the lady tried in the nicest possible way to tell her she was dreaming. "Try growing succulents like agave – they do well here." All the while thinking, "You poor deluded dumb emigrant. Imagine trying to grow roses by the beach! Salt spray, hot sun, all the wrong conditions."

But my determined mother wasn't about to let climate, topography or weather deter her. Nor the helpful suggestions of her new neighbour. She didn't actually know what a succulent was and couldn't pronounce agave, but even if she could, these were not what she had set her heart on. Since leaving Hungary, she had been determined that one day she would have the kind of garden she remembered as a little girl when she lived in a house surrounded by roses, geraniums and fragrant flowering shrubs. Even after that house was taken from them, the smaller cottage they moved into had a pretty garden replete with carnations, roses, lilies and herbs.

She quickly set to work. The neighbours watched in amazement as she established a 1930s Eastern European garden in 1970s northern beaches Sydney. First, several car-loads of Hungarians arrived. Amid much hard slog, shouting and laughing, interspersed with frequent eating and drinking, they helped my parents remove all the original shrubs, cut down the three half dead pine trees and rip out the honeysuckle. The same jolly crew returned the following weekend to dig out the worst of the inhospitable dirt and replace it with the rich loamy soil my father had arranged to have delivered.

The third weekend was far less noisy but much more pungent. Only one of my father's friends turned up. The trailer hitched to his car was full to the brim with aged horse manure.

I have no idea how far he had transported this steaming cornucopia but suffice to say, in these days before not covering your load merited a stiff fine, you could smell him loooong before he arrived.

He dumped the lot on the driveway and then joined my parents in the satisfying task of distributing it through the garden, mixing it carefully into the soil. Neighbouring Succulent Lady and her husband looked on in horror as the three laughed and toiled – happy as pigs in mud. Or more accurately – Hungarians in pony poo.

The smell slowly dissipated over the next few weeks, helped by strong sea breezes and the salty tang of the ocean and the neighbours were eventually able to open their windows again.

Now it was time to plant! Two dozen rose bushes – crimson, yellow, white. Interspersed with lavender bushes and leggy carnation plants. The roses were purchased from the nursery, but all the other plants were cuttings taken from the gardens of friends. All lovingly watered and nurtured.

Like the then Prince of Wales, my mother was a firm believer in talking to plants. How else could they understand what was expected of them? She held long conversations with them, often in the early evening when she watered. My paternal grandfather had done the same but there the similarity in their gardening methods ended. Unlike my grandfather, my mother did not coerce or threaten the flora.

There is no doubt that my grandfather had a real knack for gardening. It was a well-known fact that he could grow just about anything. Anywhere. What was not so well-known was that he bullied his plants into thriving. Treating his garden like his own personal battalion, he was a ruthless commander and had absolutely no compunction in court-marshalling then executing anything that failed to measure up to his exacting standards.

According to family lore, his methods were simple. Immediately after planting and watering in, he addressed the new recruit directly. "Right – you have three weeks. Or out you come!"

At the end of each day, he would remind the plant – politely but firmly – that time was marching on. At the beginning of the final week, he made it very clear that the day of judgement was fast approaching. And as soon as the three weeks was up – any shrub, bush, herb or seedling that showed signs of wilting or not yet starting to grow roots was for the chop. Or more accurately – the compost heap.

Occasionally when he was feeling mellow, he might grant a stay of execution if a plant was clearly trying its best, adding another week or two before sentence was pronounced and mercilessly carried out. It appeared to work. He had a flourishing garden filed with thoroughly chastened, extremely well-behaved horticulture.

My mother's approach couldn't have been more different. She coaxed, cossetted and nurtured her garden. Regularly watered, fed every 12 months with dynamic lifter and spoken to lovingly most evenings, every single plant repaid her efforts. Her rose bushes produced fragrant heavy blooms, carnation stems drooped with frilly flowers and her annuals were a riot of colour every season.

She established a magnificent veggie patch in the back garden. Not measuring more than three metres square, lettuce, carrots, onions, potatoes and a variety of herbs grew in neat rows. Around the perimeter sturdy trellises held tomato vines, beans and peas while in each corner, she planted lemon, lime, orange and grapefruit trees. The rest of the back garden consisted of lawn apart from an avocado tree and a banana palm, over which she and the many resident possums waged ongoing war.

When they first moved to the area and once the bones of the garden were established, my father was content for my mother to take over this aspect of their life. Dad was more than willing to mow the lawn, trim bushes and generally follow my mother's instructions. The garden was her domain. His was the house. He would not have thought to question her decisions any more than she would have interfered with his mending of fences, painting of guttering and general handy-man tasks. His relationship with the garden was akin to a Victorian father's affection for his children – he loved it, was proud of it but had no desire to be involved emotionally. Although according to my grandmother, having watched his own father storm about instilling fear and trepidation as he yelled at his garden, my father feared that gardening would be too emotionally demanding.

Although my mother presided over the garden like an enlightened, loving potentate, she would have been delighted to share her throne with her spouse. In the early days, she often sat him down to discuss what she wanted to tackle next. He would smile and nod (most people wisely did that when confronted with my mother's at times terrifyingly full-on enthusiasm) but he really did not want to commit. Happy to be involved in the planting but never the planning was how he once described his role.

This division of labour worked well for them and their garden was universally admired by all the neighbours and friends. Several years after moving there, they demolished the beach house and built a modern two-storey home, with sliding doors opening onto wide balconies to take in the panoramic views.

The day before demolition, my mother prepared a delicious afternoon tea for the builder and his team. But as they tucked into her cookies and cakes, no doubt thinking what a lovely lady she was, she laid it on the line. The garden was to be protected at ALL COSTS. Not ONE rose bush, petunia, tomato plant, soil covered carrot crown was to be damaged during demolition and building. She didn't add, "Or else!" She didn't need to. She could look very ferocious when she chose, even when handing around walnut cake. She asked them to promise. They promised.

And to the amazement of every one of their friends and acquaintances who had ever suffered the – apparently inevitable – destruction of a garden during the renovation/building cycle, they kept their promise. The garden survived intact. It was even rumoured that the carpenter was seen pulling weeds out of the vegie patch, but no-one believed that.

A big new house gave my father even more handyman chores to occupy his fairly limited free time while my mother continued to devote herself to the garden. Every so often, she tried to involve him in her more detailed horticultural plans, but he resisted manfully. So, it came as a lovely surprise when one fine day, dad announced he had put his name down on the waiting list of the local Diggers' Club.

Though 'announced'" is not an accurate description. He played that special game married people play when they really want to do something but suspect their spouse really won't want them to do it. So, they sort of ask. And they sort of tell. Then according to the unwritten but no less immutable Rules of Marriage, if their significant other doesn't actually leap up and yell, "Over my dead body!" or words to that effect, they will forever be reminded that they said it was ok.

My mother thought dad joining the Diggers' Club was more than just ok. She thought it was a wonderful idea. Although she didn't understand why membership was limited to men, she almost fell over herself in her enthusiasm for him to become a member of – the local gardening club.

What a great way for him to catch up with friends while discussing the merits of blood and bone versus dynamic lifter! The impressive premises were located a short walk from their home – another big tick. And when she heard that it had a bar – a huge room on the ocean side of the building, with spectacular views of the surf, she knew it was the perfect place for him to spend his leisure hours.

She began entertaining great hopes for the gardening future of their marriage. Once dad caught the bug from fellow male gardening enthusiasts, she could see the two of them contentedly poring over rose catalogues, spending many delightful hours together strolling through garden centres and after dinner, discussing the merits of lavender as opposed to English Box. She had always known that deep inside her beloved husband, there lurked the traditional Hungarian love of gardening. He had just been too busy and distracted to indulge. But now – in the company of other men, relaxing with beer in hand, watching the surf roll in, it would all come bubbling forth.

Sadly, it was not to be. A few months later, having had his membership seconded by several neighbours, dad was accepted into the fold and set off for his first visit. He invited my mother to go along and didn't quite understood why she insisted he go alone. She said it was so he could, "Get to know the other members." He thought that was very nice of her and he headed out happily.

I happened to call in an hour or so after he left. My mother could hardly wait to tell me where he was.

"Your father has gone to a gardening lecture!" she announced. "At the Diggers' Club. He's just joined!"

I almost choked on my coffee. Looking at her happy smile, her glowing eyes, I thought – oh help, she really has got the wrong end of the shovel this time. Someone needs to sort this out. I just wish it didn't have to be me!

"Mum," I began tentatively. "Dad's gone to the Diggers' Club, right? The place around the corner? What makes you think it's a gardening club?"

"Diggers' Club, darling. Diggers. You know. Digging. Gardening." Making digging motions with her arms and speaking clearly and very slowly, she gave me a concerned look. Obviously, I was not firing on all cylinders and needed careful handling.

Taking a big deep breath, I prepared to burst her bubble.

"Mum, the Diggers' Club is not a gardening club. It's a – well – it's a social club. For men. With alcohol and poker machines and probably a gym. But definitely no seed packets or fruit trees."

"What! Then why call it a Diggers' Club?"

"You know – Diggers. Slang for Australian soldier. It's an RSL Club. Returned Servicemen's League. Think ANZAC Day," I suggested helpfully.

She didn't want to think ANZAC Day. She loved ANZAC Day but right now it was the last thing on her mind.

"So, it's not a gardening club? It's a drinking club! A poker machine club! A… a MEN'S club!" she declared angrily.

Having had her dream of a gardening-club-member husband so cruelly snatched from her, she was now travelling with lightning speed right into a 'Sordid Strip Joint with Optional S&M on Fridays' scenario. Her imagination was moving so fast, I could almost hear the whooshing sound.

Before she beat her breast and cried, "How could he do this to me!" I needed to haul her back from Lunatic-Ville into the Land of Sane People.

"I really don't think Dad tried to deceive you, Mum. Did he ever say it was a gardening club?"

"He said he wanted to join the Diggers' Club."

"Yup. And he has. Except not the one you thought he joined."

An hour or so later, the newest Diggers' Club affiliate returned home, totally unaware of the drama that had unfolded during his absence. He had that contented glow men get after a few cleansing ales and a whiskey or two.

"How was the CLUB?" my mother asked, refusing to dignify it with a name, especially this most misleading one. Her tone was distinctly unfriendly, but he didn't seem to notice.

"Fabulous! Really nice members. Lovely clubhouse and a terrific bar. I think I'm going to like it. A lot."

Fixing him with an ice glare, my mother stormed into the kitchen. Confused – as well he might be – dad turned to me.

"What was that all about? I thought she was glad I'd joined!"

"Don't worry Dad. Mum is just disappointed you didn't join a gardening club."

"Why would I join a gardening club? That's your mother's idea of a good time, not mine!"

Helen – happy gardening.

Otto – happy not gardening.

Recipe for Lángos

Ingredients

600 g plain flour

500 ml slightly warmed milk. Be careful – if it's too hot, the yeast won't rise

1 sachet dried yeast (7 gms)

7 gms salt

Plus oil for frying – olive oil is best but canola also works

Garlic to rub on top

Method

- Mix yeast into warm milk in a large bowl. Leave for about 10 minutes until frothy

- Mix in flour and salt with wooden spoon until just combined

- Turn out onto floured board and knead it until it forms a smooth slightly elastic ball

- Place dough ball back into bowl and leave in warm place to rise for about 30 minutes. It should double in size.

- NB - in summer - DO NOT place it in the hot sun. It will morph into a sinister, tasteless, hollow ball of mush!

- Once it has risen, divide into 8 pieces (6 if you want bigger Lángos)

- Roll each piece on floured board into squares - about 2cm thick.

- Heat oil until a small cube of bread sizzles when thrown in

- Fry each piece until it is golden brown – it won't take more than a few seconds. Turn over and fry other side.

- Remove and keep warm while you fry the rest.

- Traditionally served with only garlic rubbed on the top and sprinkling of salt and paprika. But sour cream and sprinkling of chopped chives is also nice.

CHAPTER 12
Strudel Wars or Rétes Rivalry

(*rétes* pronounced rae-tash)

If Grudge Holding ever becomes an Olympic sport, Hungary's finest will climb the podium every four years to collect gold, silver, bronze or possibly all three. The national ability to never, ever, ever let bygones be bygones is as well developed as its collective ear for music, creative use of pithy swear words and irrepressible black humour. Hungary has hated some countries such as Serbia and Turkey for a very long time. Others like Russia (in both its imperial and Soviet iterations) are relatively newcomers to the We Will Never Stop Loathing You List.

While I believe Hungary's antipathy to Russia is and always will be of the 24 carat Gold! Gold! Gold! Variety, its relationship with nearest neighbour Austria is more nuanced. It probably belongs in the Silver or even Bronze medal class of grudge bearing. This animosity can be traced back almost five centuries, which only goes to prove that not only don't Hungarians forgive, they also have very long memories.

Before the sixteenth century, Hungary or more correctly the Kingdom of the Magyars, had kicked along pretty well with its Habsburg neighbour. Its main problem was the Turks. They had been fighting them off and on for years, only to be completely annihilated in the Battle of Mohács. A pivotal moment not just for the Magyars but Europe as a whole because it opened the way to the Ottoman Empire's expansion. The date of the battle – 29 August 1526 – is etched in the collective Hungarian psyche. Facing its enemy on the swampy marshland near the town of Mohács, the Hungarians force was led by their beloved King Louis II. Known in Hungarian as *Nagy Lajos* – Big Louis – this makes him sound more like a high-ranking member of the Mafia than the wise, scholarly ruler he was. Numbering over 60,000 armed-to-the-hilt men, the Turkish army was almost twice the size of the Hungarian. Each Turks was also twice the size of each Magyar, so it was never going to end well.

The Turkish commander was Sultan Süleyman the Magnificent. This title was not just good PR – Süleyman was a superb tactician and brilliant strategist whose penchant for skinning alive any of his soldiers who didn't fight to the death guaranteed him dedicated manpower although probably not unbridled affection. To make it even less of a fair contest, the invaders possessed large numbers of cannons. Against this mighty enemy, the Hungarian cavalry, superb horsemen though they were, didn't stand a chance.

Early in the battle, Big Louis was thrown from his horse and killed; a merciful fate compared to the treatment Süleyman usually handed out to vanquished monarchs. The leaderless Magyar army was quickly defeated. Even more significantly, Louis left no heirs and so without a king to lead and unify, Hungary ceased to exist as an autonomous entity. Following a long, bloody civil war, in 1547 the entire southern and central part of the country was annexed by the Turks and incorporated into the vast Ottoman Empire that continued to spread its tentacles across Europe.

To make matters even worse, the northern part of the country, richly forested with prime agricultural land, ceded from the Magyars to become the Kingdom of Transylvania. Knowing it could not survive alone, this new kingdom formed an alliance with the remaining Hungarian provinces in the east of the country. Busy consolidating their conquered territory by massacring as many people as possible, the Turks allowed this new kingdom to remain an independent principality within its empire.

Galvanised into action by the Ottoman threat now lurking on their own doorstep, the Austrian Habsburgs finally threw their hats into the ring. In 1551 they succeeded in defeating Süleyman's army in a major battle that drove the Turks out of Transylvania. But in what was to become a pattern in Hungarian history, once the task was completed, the liberators didn't just congratulate themselves on a job well done, wash their hands, pack up their weapons and depart. They stayed on and established their own dominion. For the next 150 years, the ancient Magyar homeland was divided into three separate kingdoms. Only the northern section of the country remaining truly Hungarian, ruled by the hereditary kings of Hungary. Transylvania remained part of the Habsburg Empire and the rest of the country continued to belong to the Ottoman empire. Complicated? Yes.

A concerted effort was not made to expel the Turks from the whole of Europe until 1686. Led by the Holy Roman Emperor, blessed and prayed over by Pope Innocent XI, the enormous Army of Christ set off to defeat the Infidel once and for all. After many bloody battles and over one and a half million lives lost, at the end of the 17th century it finally succeeded.

But after the shouting died down and the blood dried on the battlefields, the Hungarians faced a bleak, uncertain future. Almost two thirds of the ethnic population had perished during the Turkish occupation, leaving large parts of the country totally uninhabited. So, the ruling Habsburgs initiated a massive Populate or Perish Campaign – carting in huge numbers of ethnic German, Slovakian, Romanian and Croatian families to settle the decimated areas, thus further consolidating Austrian influence. Having survived the Mongol occupation in the 13th century and weathered a century and a half of brutal Turkish occupation, the proud ancient land of Attila again found itself subservient. This time to the Austrians.

Hungary was treated like a province of Austria. Ethnic Hungarians enjoyed few personal freedoms and even fewer political rights. Only the richest landowners – often affiliated by marriage to Austrian aristocracy – held any power. For the rest of the fiercely patriotic nationalistic population, such subservience was intolerable. Fuelled by underground independence movements (and probably illicit home-brewed *palinka*), revolts erupted with monotonous regularity. Just as quickly, they were brutally and efficiently suppressed.

This 'Rise Up/Get Slapped Down' czardas went on for years. It was only during the widespread European revolutions of 1848 that the Hungarians came close to regaining their national independence. Much better led and organised, several initially separate revolts rapidly escalated into nation-wide revolution and for a while, it looked as if they would succeed in getting rid of the hated Habsburgs. Hungarian autonomy finally appeared within reach, but it was not to be. In an uncharacteristically shrewd move, the Austrian emperor Franz I approached Tsar Nicholas I of Russia for assistance. Worried the fledgling 'let's throw off our oppressors' movement would spread to Russia's own territories such as Poland, the Tsar promptly dispatched several thousand elite Russian troops into Hungary. The combined military power of two mighty dynasties eventually succeeded in putting down the revolution.

Hungary was plunged into mourning, not only for its thwarted liberal ambitions but for the many idealistic young men who had died. As well as the tens of thousands of commoners killed in the fighting or the aftermath, every single noble Hungarian family suffered and the cream of Hungary's aristocracy faced the gallows or life-long exile for their part in the uprising. This was the bitterest blow yet. Hungary was placed under martial law and although an uneasy peace settled over the country, the Hungarians continued to agitate for independence.

Austria was never going to cut her loose – she was too dependent on Hungary's agriculture, forests, mines, manpower. But it became increasingly clear that the status quo could not continue, and concessions had to be granted. Known by his Austrian subjects as the Imbecile Emperor (and I'm guessing this was not a compliment) Franz I again showed he had more brains than they gave him credit for. Realising he could not bring about the drastic changes that were needed, he abdicated in favour of his 18-year-old nephew Franz Joseph.

It was a wise decision. The new emperor possessed everything his uncle lacked – prodigious energy, intelligence, a highly developed work ethic, popularity, good looks, patience, two functioning eyes. Sadly, in addition to being competent and reliable, Franz Joseph was mind-numbingly pedestrian, boring and predictable. But his Austrians subjects decided this was a very small price to pay and over the next 68 years, Franz Joseph's steady hand on the tiller of empire guaranteed them prosperity and security.

While Austrian troops continued to occupy Hungary, the young emperor settled into the Hofburg Palace in Vienna, where he shared the vast imperial apartments with his formidable mother Archduchess Sophie. Sleeping on a narrow camp bed amid all the gilding, brocade and splendour, the most eligible bachelor in the world lived a Spartan, regulated existence. Archduchess Sophie, nicknamed 'the Only Man in the Hofburg' during the reign of the previous emperor, was determined to continue playing an important role in government. Loving her son and wanting above all else for him to succeed in the lofty position to which he had been elevated (in no small measure due to her efforts), she tended to be overly generous with her advice and suggestions. Some of the time, her beloved Franzie took her advice and sometimes he didn't. It was ever thus...

Meanwhile, the cost of keeping Hungary a veritable armed camp was proving extremely draining both economically and militarily. This was not lost on Franz Joseph. Although no more politically progressive than his uncle had been and in the face of almost universal opposition from his ministers, he began to think about making concessions. But the process was excruciating slow and who knows how long it would have taken him to actually grant them? But in 1854, the Emperor got lucky. And unexpectedly, so did the Hungarians.

It was the stuff of fairy-tale. At the age of 22, Franz Joseph met and fell madly in love with his 16-year-old cousin Elizabeth of Wittelsbach, an obscure Bavarian princess known as Sissi. The fact that he was supposed to woo and marry Sissi's older sister Helene only added a delicious operatic piquancy to the tale. Archduchess Sophie bitterly opposed the match, not just because her carefully laid matrimonial plans had been thwarted but because she could see trouble ahead. Although she tried to counsel her son, the usually level-headed Franz Joseph was infatuated with his lovely young cousin. Declaring himself, "As happy as a sand-boy and as much in love as a Lieutenant!" he proposed after a two-day courtship. Invisible violins played, and the romantic Austrians swooned with delight.

There is no doubt that Sissi was heart-stoppingly beautiful, charming, bewitching, delightful. But unfortunately for her besotted husband, his bride was also neurotic, moody, self-obsessed and completely unsuited to life as an Empress. Married amidst great pomp and ceremony in Vienna, Sissi very quickly regretted her mistake in her choice of life-partner. Once she had done her Imperial duty by producing several children including the all-important heir, finding the atmosphere at court almost as stultifying as her husband's personality, Sissi bolted.

To her husband's great sorrow and her Austrian subjects' increasing annoyance, the Empress spent much of the next 44 years flitting around the world, coming under the spell of passions as diverse as the Greek Islands, the poetry of Homer, the music of Wagner and the speed of English thoroughbred horses. Each passion was all-consuming while it lasted, only to be rapidly replaced by something new and equally compelling. Except for one passion. The greatest love of Sissi's life and the only one that would not eventually disappoint her. Hungary.

No one really knows what first attracted her to this most troublesome part of her husband's vast empire but from the very first time she accompanied Franz Joseph on a visit, she was smitten. She loved its people – for which her Viennese subjects never forgave her. She loved its sweeping landscapes from the vast Carpathian plain to the rugged mountains of Tihony. She soon learned to speak fluent, accent-less Hungarian (no mean feat) and immersed herself in Hungarian poetry, literature, history and art. So, it was probably inevitable that the Empress of Austria, by this time widely acknowledged to be the most beautiful woman in the world, would become devoted to the cause closest to Hungarian hearts – national independence.

At the time it was rumoured that several politically influential, immensely wealthy and – it must be said, handsome and dashing – Hungarian aristocrats also got a wee bit too close to her heart – especially Count Géza Andrássy. But this is most unlikely. Elizabeth saw Hungary as her raison d'être, her sacred calling and – much to the consternation of her husband and increasingly vocal disapproval of the entire Austrian Court – she became Hungary's greatest advocate. When Count Andrássy led a group of his aristocratic countrymen in pushing for greater Hungarian autonomy, Elizabeth championed their cause both publicly and more importantly – privately. Still very much in love with his wife, frustrated and enchanted by turns, Franz Joseph finally gave in. The outcome was the creation of a Dual Monarchy – the Austro-Hungarian Empire – with Hungary granted equal status to Austria.

In 1867, Franz Joseph was crowned King of Hungary. Elizabeth became Queen on the day she described as, "The happiest of my entire life!" No wonder the Austrians were miffed. Three years later, Pest, Buda and the ancient city of OBuda were amalgamated to form Budapest, giving Hungary not just a stunning new queen but a stunning new capital city.

The Hungarians repaid Elizabeth's love. They idolised her, naming bridges, streets, suburbs, monuments, new-born babies (usually, though not always, girls) after her. To this day, portraits of Sissi decorate public buildings, having been retrieved from wherever they were secreted during the bleak Soviet years. Even in the 21st century, new statues of Sissi are regularly unveiled in Budapest, amidst much fanfare and nostalgia.

When the empress was murdered in 1898 – stabbed in the heart by an anarchist as she walked along a quay in Geneva – the whole of Hungary plummeted into a Death of Diana-like avalanche of grief. Grown men wept in public. Distraught women flooded the churches and in Parliament, the usually poker-faced Prime Minister Baron Dezső Bánffy delivered her eulogy with tears running down his cheeks. It was the end of an era. Never again would Hungary have a champion as influential, as loving or as devoted.

The Dual Monarchy limped on, outwardly alive but inwardly mortally wounded, much like the Old Emperor. The regime had become rotten at its core. True equality continued to elude Hungary as Austria retained much of the political although not economic power and only loyalty to Franz Joseph kept the partnership viable. Composing waltzes, building palaces and cooking delicious food, the two countries remained shackled together until November 1918. Ethnic rivalry expressed itself through vying to create the most melodious waltzes and serve up the most sumptuous food.

Culinary competition was especially fierce. Nowhere more so than in relation to the delicious dessert/cake/sweet/roll – STRUDEL. How to cook it. Who invented it. Even what to call it. In Hungary it is called *Rétes* (pronounced rae-tash – meaning 'layered'). As a child I asked my grandmother why its Hungarian name was so different to what the rest of the world called it. I found it hard to argue with the logic of her response, "Because we invented it!"

In the same way that the English and Australians might debate the finer points of cricket and Germans and French might argue about pretty much everything, Hungarians and Austrians will eventually get around to the Strudel/Rétes debate, each passionately claiming they invented it, perfected it and thus own it. World without end. Amen.

As far as I can discover after extensive research accompanied by much strudel/*rétes* eating, they are both right. And both wrong. Strudel was invented in Vienna in the 1690s by one of the pastry chefs who served up delectable meals at the Hofburg Palace. So, Vienna = Austria = tick. But wait for it – the clever little cook(ie) was Hungarian. He named it *rétes*, due to its many layers. So = Hungary = Tick. Tick. And Tick.

Rétes featured prominently in my family's food repertoire with my mother and grandmother trying to out-*rétes* each other. Delicious apple and cinnamon, crunchy walnut, rich dark poppy-seed and sultana, luscious cherry *rétes* appeared regularly as well as caramelised cabbage and black pepper – a savoury offering every bit as delectable as the sweet ones. My mother's *rétes* was unfailingly delicious – beautifully crisp outer layers enfolding soft, ambrosial filling. But if I'm now allowed to state my preference – and as a child this was not always such a wise idea – I thought my grandmother's *rétes* was even better because she Made. Her. Own. Puff. Pastry.

By the time my parents arrived in Australia, although it was possible to buy thick refrigerated slabs of puff pastry from exclusive Delicatessens (remember those?) to make *rétes*, this still had to be thawed and rolled out to requisite thinness. It was quite a physically demanding task and produced more than acceptable results.

But I loved watching my grandmother make it from scratch – rigorous measuring, mixing, kneading, resting, more kneading and then rolling it out as thinly as possible to cover the entire table. And what she did next was akin to alchemy. Placing her hands carefully under the already paper-thin sheet of shiny, buttery pastry, incredibly gently and slowly she pulled and stretched and worked the pastry towards her with outspread fingers. Moving patiently around the large kitchen table, she painstakingly attacked it from every side until finally an almost transparent, glossy film lay like a table cloth over the special table cloth that was reserved for this purpose. Once she was satisfied the pastry was thin enough, she cut it into *rétes* size rectangles and layered six lengths on top of each other, ready to be filled and rolled up for baking. The entire process took the best part of a day but the results! Light, crisp, sublime.

If it tore while being stretched, this labour of love would take even longer because then the pastry had to be gathered together, kneaded, rolled and stretched all over again. It was delicate, stressful work. My grandmother once confessed to me that when she was a little girl, she occasionally tormented her own mother by surreptitiously pinching a tiny hole in the pastry while it rested waiting for the magic pulling. This would of course cause the pastry to tear, forcing the poor woman to begin the entire process from scratch. I considered this the height of wickedness and was filled with admiration at her daring.

When I grew up and started to cook, although I never contemplated undergoing this culinary version of water-torture, I often made *rétes* using the now readily available filo pastry. For dinner parties, I always referred to this sweet centre-piece by its correct name, only to be rewarded with blank looks followed by the inevitable, "Oh you made strudel!" Actually, no. I didn't.

It's not simply patriotism that makes me declare Austrian strudel is not as good as Hungarian *rétes*. I think there is a something inauthentic about the Austrian offering and I speak from experience having eaten it (probably far more frequently than is good for me) in Vienna, Graz, Innsbruck and Salzburg.

I have a special fondness for Salzburg. It is the first Austrian city my parents visited after they escaped across the Hungarian border in 1956. Like several thousand other refugees at the time, they were living in a Red Cross Displaced Persons' Camp near the lovely hilltop town of Melk. Dormitory accommodation in freezing tin sheds, communal bathrooms, institutional food and cramped conditions but still so much better than the horrors they had left behind. The (mostly young) people relished their new freedom. One day, the wonderful Red Cross even took them on a day trip – by bus to Salzburg. For my classical music obsessed father, it was on par with a visit to paradise.

Mozart's birthplace. Encircled by distant mountains, this charming city with narrow cobbled streets, verdant green parks and beautifully preserved 17th century architecture was as wonderful as they had dared imagine. They climbed the steep stairs of the Festungsberg up to Nonnberg Abbey – an 8th century Benedictine edifice perched eagle-like above the rooftops. My mother lit a candle in the vaulted white marble interior, giving thanks for their escape and praying for those left behind.

Down in the city again, the group was left alone to explore. My father made his own pilgrimage to No. 9 Getreidegasse, one of the many elegant apartment houses set around a courtyard. Leopold Mozart, a musician in the Salzberger Royal Chamber (court orchestra), his wife Maria and their family lived here from 1747 to 1773. It was here on 27 January 1756 that Maria gave birth to their seventh child. They christened the baby Johannes Chrysostomus Wolfgangus Theophilus Amadeus Mozart, although they wisely shortened it to Wolfgang Amadeus.

A museum since the mid-19th century, this shrine to the great composer charged an entrance fee, thus making it unaffordable for my parents, who like their fellow refugees didn't have a 'bean to bless themselves with' as the old saying goes. But just seeing the building, stroking the panelling of the front door and standing on the worn marble doorstep was enough for my father.

Not far from Getreidegasse is the Old Town with some of Salzburg's best cafés, including the historic Café Tomaselli. Sadly, like the museum, you needed money to fully participate in the Austrian café experience. But peering inside from the alleyway cost nothing and my parents passed a happy few minutes doing just that. They didn't feel bitter or deprived. They had great faith that with hard work and dedication, one day they would be able to afford all the good things that eluded them at the time. And right now, they had their hard-won freedom and that was worth all the coffee, cake and whipped cream in the world.

Before being bused home that afternoon, the tired but happy refugees enjoyed yet another example of the kindness of their Austrian hosts – a meal of wurst (Austrian sausage) sweet mustard and fresh bread. A huge treat and a fitting end to their special day out.

Two decades later my parents returned to Salzburg. Australia had been good to them and although they were not wealthy, they could now afford regular trips back to Europe. Hand in hand they retraced their steps. They again climb up to Nonnberg, where my mother lit another candle and then wound their way slowly back down into the city. They walked for hours, visited every room in the Mozart Museum and finally ended up in the Old Town. Café Tomaselli beckoned. This time they went in, had coffee, cake and for good measure, a large cognac each. My father left a generous tip. They were very happy – some things were worth waiting for.

I was in my mid-20s when I first made it to Salzburg. It was still the elegant city my parents had fallen in love with in 1957 but with a major difference. Tourists no longer flocked here to honour the musical prodigy with the phenomenal memory and complicated Christian names. For most people Salzburg now meant a disobedient nun running through breathtaking scenery, racing wimple-less down the mountain to the Abbey and arriving late for mass. It meant stern, whistle-blowing (although admittedly very handsome) Captain Von Trapp, his seven adorable musically gifted curtain-clad children and three-plus hours of ear-worm tunes.

OK, I love the *Sound of Music* as much as anybody and probably more than most men out there. I admit to seeing it multiple times over the years and at one (admittedly low) point in my life I could recite all the lyrics and much of the dialogue. But if I am to be achingly honest, I have always thought it a great pity that Salzburg had gone from being worshipped as Mozart's birthplace to Von Trapp-Ville, most famous for being the setting of this romanticised and let's face it – geographically incorrect melodrama. I mean hello! That last poignant trek across the alps to freedom? Captain, Maria, children – if you keep Climbing Every Mountain with your faces stoically pointed in that direction, you will end up crossing the border into – NAZI GERMANY! An extremely bad career move on every level.

But determined to cash in on SOM fame (and who can really blame it), Salzburg shamelessly sold out to Twentieth Century Fox. Every tourist office offered Von Trapp Tours. Every location used in the movie had life-size cardboard cut-outs of the characters. Everywhere, delighted (demented?) fans ran amok, flinging their arms around while singing about Does, Female Dears and A Drink with Jam and Bread as they danced around the fountain in the Mirabelle Gardens. Most of them were much older than Sixteen Going on Seventeen and should have known better, in my humble opinion.

The restaurants and cafés also got in on the act, serving Von Trapp Salad, Captain Cider and Schnitzel with Noodles. There was no escaping from it.

Having spent the day dodging warbling tourists, I decided to treat myself to lunch at Café Tomaselli. This was one of the oldest cafés in Salzburg and had even been frequented by the

Mozart family, or so it was rumoured. But if you thought – as I did – that this association would spare it from SOM fever, you would be wrong. The interior looked authentically 18th century with beautiful walnut panelling and polished brass fittings and I breathed a sigh of relief as I sank into a cosy red velvet banquette to examine the menu. Alongside the traditional offerings like *Schwarzwalder Kirschtorte* (Black Forest cherry cake) and *Linzer Torte* (shortbread with fruit preserve on top) they offered various strudels. I ordered coffee and apple strudel and sat back to indulge. When it arrived, the pretty porcelain plate was covered with a paper napkin on which was printed Crisp Apple Strudel! and the first two verses of My Favourite Things.

To add insult to injury, the strudel wasn't – crisp that is. And completely the wrong shape and texture. Not a light, fragrant log-shaped concoction, oozing apple and cinnamon filling. This pseudo strudel was a squashy, flattish slab of filled pastry, hidden under a huge dollop of sweetened whipped cream. More of a pie and deserving no more than 5 out of 10 on my Strudel Scale/*Rétes* Ratings.

Admittedly, I've had much better, more authentic strudel in Vienna, especially at Demels. Demels's strudel was light, crisp and delicious – ranking 8 or even 8.5 on the Strudel Scale. But it still wasn't *rétes*. For that, you need to go to Hungary.

Originally called *Kave Haz* (literal translation coffee house) cafés have been an important part of Budapest's culture since the mid-19th century. The first and for many years the most famous was *Ruszwurm*, opened in 1827. Still going strong, sadly it is now packed with tourists looking for the traditional Hungarian *Kave Haz* experience. Which pretty much guarantees they aren't getting it.

But authentic cafés continue to abound. Here the coffee is black as pitch and strong enough to make an elephant levitate and the freshly baked offerings have been the death of many a diet. And probably many a dieter. It is not unusual for a typical Hungarian cake like *Dobos Torte* (drum cake) to contain vast quantities of eggs, cream, butter, sugar, more cream, more sugar, more butter. Health food it definitely isn't but many Hungarians believe giving up indulgences like alcohol and cake doesn't actually make you live longer – it only makes it seems longer. So, they tuck in.

It's relatively easy to find an authentic café in Budapest or anywhere else in Hungary for that matter. If the menu lists strudel, step away now. But if it features *rétes*, it means that somewhere in the depths of the kitchen there is someone who values Hungarian cuisine above tourist income. However, if the *rétes* is served with a big dollop of whipped cream a la Vienne, this café is sitting on the Should We Sell Out to Tourists? Fence and they need to immediately dismount on one side or the other. The only accompaniment an authentic piece of *rétes* needs is a light dusting of icing sugar. And a second piece of *rétes*.

Among the best *rétes* I've ever had since my grandmother died (sorry mum but it's true) was at the Muvész Café on Andrássy Ut. This nineteenth century café is very popular with tourists but this is reflected in the prices, not the authenticity of the food. They serve *rétes* sans cream and their *megyes rétes* ticks all the boxes. Slightly tart cherries with sweet toasted breadcrumbs in a light flaky pastry is sublime and worthy of 9/10 on the *Rétes* Ratings.

The best *rétes* I've had since the days I watched my grandmother stretch the pastry while I defied my inner demons to give it just the tiniest of pinches, was in a hole in the wall café in Budapest's Jewish Quarter.

This is one of my favourite parts of Budapest. Once the scene of unimaginable horror during the brutal Nazi years, in the past 10 years or so, the Jewish Quarter has re-emerged as the hippest, most vibrant part of this hip vibrant city. Situated right in the centre of the Quarter is *Gozsdu-udvar* (Gozsdu Courtyard) – a complex of seven interlinked buildings and courtyards opening onto three streets. Built in 1901 by a Jewish charitable organisation from money left to it from the estate of wealthy financier Emánuel Gozsdu, it was intended to provide housing for the city's Jewish population close to the enormous Main Synagogue.

From November 1944 to January 1945 the complex was part of the Jewish Ghetto, when many thousands of people were crammed into apartments designed to accommodate hundreds. The total Jewish population of Budapest was around 200,000 in 1943 but less than 70,000 remained alive by the time the Russians 'liberated' the city in May 1945.

Many of the buildings of *Gozsdu-udvar* were badly damaged and left derelict for almost half a century. In 1999 the complex was privatised during the heady days immediately after the Soviet Union packed up and finally buggered off. After extensive renovation work, in 2009 *Gozsdu-udvar* re-opened and the numerous restaurants, bars, cafés, shops and courtyards quickly became the hub of the city's nightlife.

Yet despite the noise and buzzy vibe, the memory of what happened here is ever present in the Jewish Quarter. On *Dob Ut* (Drum Street) the Carl Lutz Memorial commemorates the Swiss diplomat who issued false documents and set up 74 'Safe Houses' in a desperate attempt to thwart the Nazi killing-machine in the final days of the regime. A life-size bronze angel rides down a cascading wave, reaching her hand out to the figure collapsed on the ground. Above the angel's head are words from the Talmud, "Whoever saves one life is considered to have saved the entire world."

Less prominent but no less poignant, down towards the Danube between the lines of bricks of one of the outside walls of the Faculty of Arts Building at the Eötvös Loránd University, a narrow barely noticeable bronze strip contains the names of Jewish teachers and students who perished. It takes some effort to find it but once you do, it is impossible to look away.

The terrible loss of life is right under your feet – literally. Spread along the streets of the Jewish Quarter are thousands of brass and marble plaques inserted into the footpath. Called Memory Stones, they feature the name, date of birth, year of deportation and date of death of Holocaust victims. A subtle and moving reminder of the tragedy that claimed the lives of so many ordinary people.

But without doubt the most powerful memorial is on the banks of the Danube right in front of the magnificent Parliament House in Pest. Sixty pairs of bronze shoes stand empty and abandoned, looking like they have just been taken off by their owners. Erected in 2005, it commemorates the thousands of Jewish people who were murdered here by the Nazi-supporting Hungarian Arrow Cross Party at the end of 1944. Marched down to the river at night, forced to remove their shoes before they were shot, their bodies fell into the river and were swept away. Boots, fashionable high heeled shoes, men's brogues, down at heel slippers, children's shoes and a tiny pair of baby's boots, its laces hanging down. An almost unbearable reminder of man's inhumanity to man.

Every time I see it, I am left speechless. Bereft. On one of my visits a few years ago, I arrived at about 5 o'clock on a chilly autumn afternoon. Just a few metres behind me the traffic hummed along Danube Boulevard while up on the footpath, the good citizens of Pest were making their way home. In front of me, the rays of the setting sun reflected off the river, touching the bronze shapes, making them shimmer and glow.

I headed back to my hotel through the Jewish Quarter, hoping to find a café where I could get a warm drink or better still – a strong one. I was chilled to the bone and not just because of the approaching night. I know the main streets of this part of Pest quite well, but I found myself down a cobbled side-street behind *Gozsudar Udvar*. I was completely lost, cold and weighed down by history. As I retraced my steps, trying to get back onto *Dob Utca* again, I walked by a gate leading to a small courtyard. I almost hurried past but then noticed the hand-written menu nailed to the post. Among a few other things, it offered coffee, cognac and *rétes*. Exactly what I needed – something familiar and comforting. I went inside.

Apart from a teenage couple melded together at one of the tiny tables, I was the only customer – not surprisingly after the tourist-lunch rush and before the evening onslaught. As I scanned the limited menu, I saw it was in Hungarian, with no English or German translations. I had obviously wandered right off the beaten track.

A young man materialised to take my order. When I asked, he told me they only did one type of *rétes* each day. Today was poppy-seed and sultana and I ordered it together with a small cognac. When it arrived, I was stunned. The filling was rich, dark and moist. And the pastry! The pastry was exceptional – delightfully crisp and almost translucent. It was many, many years since I had tasted *rétes* pastry as authentic as this and when I got up to leave, I left a large tip, complimenting the waiter on the quality of what I had just eaten.

He told me it was *hazi* - meaning 'of the house.' For a moment, I had a vision of a little old lady, painstakingly stretching pastry across a large table. But surely no-one did this now and home-made meant they created their own filling, encasing it in some – admittedly first class – commercial pastry? This was *rétes* now in Hungary and much strenuous rolling produced excellent results.

But this had tasted different somehow. Tasted like the past. My past.

"Home-made?" I asked. "All of it? Even the pastry?"

"Yes of course. Marta is making it now for tonight. You are welcome to come and look."

And that is how I ended up standing in the doorway of a little basement kitchen in down-town Pest, watching a young woman recreate my childhood. Placing her hands carefully under the sheet of shiny pastry and with infinite care, slowly, gently pulling and stretching and working the pastry towards her with out-spread fingers. Head bent; she was so engrossed in her task that she didn't notice me. Didn't see me brush away tears.

As I walked back outside, I felt a lightening of my soul. A sense of hope. Hungary is slowly reclaiming, acknowledging and paying homage to her history. In a city as old as Budapest, the past comes rushing at you from all sides. Often it is confronting and terrible – death and tragedy on a massive scale. But sometimes it is intensely personal – a tiny warm kitchen, the sugary scent of baking *rétes* and a woman weaving culinary magic through her fingers.

Recipe for Megyes Rétes (sour cherry rétes)

Ingredients:
This makes 1 large roll:

6 sheets filo pastry – completely thawed

1 jar Morello cherries – 680 gms

½ cup breadcrumbs

½ cup brown sugar

3 tablespoons butter

½ teaspoon cinnamon

Method:
- Preheat oven to 180 degrees (160 fan forced)

- Lay thawed filo pastry onto clean tea towel. Use another clean tea towel to cover pastry between steps as it dries out quickly. And if its dry, it will break when you roll it.

- Drain cherries in a colander until ALL the juice drains off. Then lay the cherries onto several sheets of paper towel – you need to remove as much moisture as possible.

- When the cherries are as dry as you can make them, mix together cherries, half the brown sugar and the cinnamon in a bowl. Taste it – it should be sweet but not too sweet. You can add a bit more sugar if it's not sweet enough. But remember – the breadcrumb mixture also has sugar in it.

- Fry breadcrumbs in half the butter until golden brown and crisp. Add the other half of the brown sugar and mix together well.

- Melt the rest of the butter in microwave. Using a pastry brush, brush half the top sheet of pastry with melted butter. Carefully fold it over so you can do the same to the sheet below. When you have competed all 6 sheets, repeat with the other half of the sheets.

- Evenly spread a very thin layer of fried breadcrumbs over the whole of the top sheet. As well as being delicious, the breadcrumbs soak up the cherry juice – otherwise you get soggy rétes!

- If you have any breadcrumbs left over, you can lightly sprinkle it onto the other sheet below the top sheet.

- Gently place the cherry mixture along the top – long edge – of the stacked filo pastry rectangle, leaving about 2 – 3 cm all around. Tuck in the short edges and then very carefully, using the tea towel, roll the pastry/filling into a tight log.

- Make sure the edges are tightly sealed/tucked under. Gently transfer the roll onto a baking tray, lined with baking paper. Brush top and sides generously with melted butter. Make sure the long join is on the underneath of the roll to ensure it doesn't break open while baking.

- Bake for around 30 minutes. But check at 20 minutes and then every 5 minutes after that. The filo pastry should be light to medium brown and crisp but NOT burnt.

- Remove from oven and let it cool a bit. Then slice on the diagonal – you should get round 6 – 8 slices from the roll.

- Serve dusted with icing sugar.

- And if you MUST – ice cream or cream.

CHAPTER 13
When Autumn Leaves Start to Fall

I don't know anyone who got an unexpected phone call in the middle of the night and afterwards said, "Terrific news! I'm so glad that happened!"

Pre-dawn phone calls usually deliver tidings you would rather not hear. News that changes your life and the lives of those around you and forever afterwards, you will refer to life as TB (Time Before) and TA (Time After). I have a friend who describes the feeling you get when you take such a momentous call as, "The bum falling out of your world."

My bum-falling out phone call came in March 2007, cutting through the Sunday morning silence like a knife. My mother – calling from their holiday flat in Port Macquarie – to tell me my father was dead. At 4am that morning, my dad sat up in bed, clutched his chest and died. He remained in character right to the end. Always hating what he called, 'fussing around', his death had been efficient and undramatic. Without complaint. Over in an instant. Unlike the heartache he left behind.

I felt totally numb for the first few seconds – blessed numbness that allowed me to brace myself before the sharp pain of reality slugged me. It really did feel like a physical blow, a searing punch to my heart. I wanted nothing more than to curl up in a ball, but I had to push the pain aside as best I could. My brother and I had to go to our mother, to bring her home and make all the arrangements.

But first, our daughter Amelia needed to be told. Awoken by the phone call, she was hovering uncertainly in our bedroom. My husband and I took her into bed with us and holding her tightly against me, I explained that something very sad had happened. Her beloved Otto-Papa was dead. Staring at me with her lovely grey seven-year-old eyes – so like my father's eyes I realised for the first time – she demanded to know why. I had no answer to give her.

"He can't be dead!" she protested angrily and burst into tears. "He can't be dead! I love him!" I loved him too. But this had not been enough to keep him with us.

The worst drive of my life. Five interminable hours while my brother and I made our way up the north coast to where my mother was waiting, struggling in our separate ways to come to terms with the enormity of what had happened. Unable to sit still, I defaulted into action. As soon as we left Sydney behind, I began the first of myriad tasks ahead of me – conveying the terrible news to my parents' many friends. My hands shook as I punched in each number. I possessed the unwanted power of shattering another family's peace, transforming an ordinary morning into something extraordinary and painful. Like ripples in a pond, every phone call spreading the grief wider and wider.

"Dad died this morning of a massive heart attack. John and I are on our way now to bring Mum home."

"Dad died this morning of a massive heart attack. John and I are on our way now to bring Mum home." I repeated those words and was met with mute silence, disbelief, often tears.

"Dad died this morning of a massive heart attack. John and I are on our way now to bring Mum home." No matter how many times I said it, it did not sound real. It sounded melodramatic. Facile lines from a second-rate play, delivered by an actor who would much rather be playing some other role.

I only phoned my parents' closest friends. Even that exhausting drive was not long enough to get the word out to the entire community, but I was confident that by the time we arrived at our destination, everyone would have been contacted. The devastating news passing from person to person by what we always called, "Hungarian Tom Toms."

My mother was strangely calm when we reached her, and I have never admired her courage more. That amazing courage had sustained her in the early hours of the morning when she called the ambulance and watched them go through the motions to save my father, even though they knew immediately he was beyond help. She was all packed by the time we arrived and had tidied the apartment, clinging to the familiar rituals of sweeping and washing up to keep hold of her sanity. She only broke down once – as we were preparing to leave – when she noticed Dad's glasses still on his bedside table, the book he had been reading lying open next to it.

We set off. I drove my mother in my car while John followed behind in theirs. As the coastline gave way to countryside, my mother told me about the wonderful day they had yesterday. A late breakfast on the balcony enjoying the sound and smell of the surf. Then lunch in their favourite café and a long walk on the beach. Before that, the highlight of the day – finding a special present for Amelia. Tiny pink sandals covered with sequin butterflies. "The store had run out of carry bags, so I said we would come back later, but your father insisted we bought them then and there. He kept saying they were perfect…"

I could see my father so clearly then. Making his way along the beach, meticulously walking only on wet hard sand because he hated 'the dry crumbly stuff', the little shoe box containing the glittery offering carefully cradled in his arms. He knew how much Amelia loved anything sparkly and he would have delighted in anticipating her delight. The last walk. The last gift. Pulling this image of his love around me, I clung to it through the drive home,

It was a steamy hot day. As the kilometres turned over, I kept remembering similar car trips as a child. Summer holidays; my father driving and my mother handing out Extra Strong Peppermints every few kilometres while my brother and I squirmed around in the back seat, trying to torment each other without being seen.

At mum's insistence, we stopped at the picnic ground at Bulahdelah where for over 30 years they had always broken the journey on their way up north. Leading me over to the picnic table and bench, "We always sat here and drank our coffee," she told me, maybe trying to accept that they never would again.

We arrived back to the house they had left only days earlier. I held my mother's hand as we went up the stairs together into their bedroom. She sat on the bed and said quietly, "I loved him so much." Finally, we were able to cry.

My brother arrived soon after, followed by my husband and Amelia. On my daughter's insistence, they had brought our dog with them. "Papa loves Sophie," Amelia explained. And Sophie loved Papa – that wonderful source of rambling walks and forbidden treats. "Dad – dogs don't eat cake!" I'd remonstrate. "This one does," he'd grin, tossing her another mouthful.

They say dogs have a sixth sense and I believe it now. The moment Sophie came inside, she ran straight upstairs into my parent's bedroom. Standing by my father's side of the bed, she howled and howled.

"Sophie is crying for Otto-Papa," said Amelia tearfully.

For the next three days, the house was filled with Dad's presence. We all noticed it and it helped us get through the painful tasks. As we sat in the kitchen drinking yet another cup of coffee, the door from the garage would open and then close gently. "Otto-Papa wants a cup!" Amelia joked, with the blessed resilience of children. On at least two occasions, Dad's favourite cap fell off the hook in the hallway. It truly did seem as if he was still here among us – urging us to get on with things – and giving us the strength to do so.

The Hungarian contingent visited and although I could see my mother found it exhausting – telling the story of how he died over and over again – she drew great comfort from these dear friends. They had all lived through so much tragedy and heartbreak, both before coming to Australia and afterwards. Having walked their own personal roads to Calvary, they now held my mother in their arms as she made the same journey.

How wholeheartedly they mourned! Sitting for hours, reminiscing about my father – funny stories and sad ones. Saying how much they loved him, how much he meant to them, how greatly they would miss him. Men and women alike – such an honest outpouring of grief. Men in their 70s openly talking of love and loss, tears in their eyes and on their cheeks. It should have been embarrassing but it wasn't. It was touching, generous, affirming. Running back and forth to the kitchen making cups of coffee, bringing in clean wine glasses and cake plates, I felt it pour over me like healing balm.

Sitting with my mother one night after the last guest had left, I asked her, "Does it hurt you, hearing them talk about Dad like that? Talking about him yourself?"

"Of course, we talk about him! There is an old Hungarian saying, *Csak az hal meg, akiről nem beszélnek.* Only he who is not spoken of really dies."

I understood then. However painful it was to talk about my father, it was the only way we could keep him tethered to us. And keeping him as part of all our lives was the greatest, bravest manifestation of love. Yes, it hurt, so very much, but we must not cut him loose.

"If I loved you less, I could talk about it more." I suddenly remembered Mr Darcy saying to Elizabeth Bennett at the end of *Pride and Prejudice* when, overcoming the social disparity between them, he professes his love. Yet even in the height of passion, he is a man of few words and tightly controlled emotion. A combination I had once considered incredibly romantic.

Yes, that was one kind of love – embraced, some may say rather too enthusiastically, by the Anglo-Saxon world. And here was another kind – heart on sleeve, demonstrative and sincere. When I die, I want to be mourned like this, I decided at that moment. Wildly. Exuberantly, tearfully, honestly. I want people who really knew me to speak of my essence. Not so much what I did but who I was. To celebrate my life and profess their love – to 'talk about it more' with tears and stories. With strong coffee, delicious cake, good wine, fine cognac. Just as we were doing with my father.

During the week that followed, I organised my first funeral and wrote my first eulogy, sincerely hoping it would be the last time I ever had to do this. I realise now it was a blessing not to be able to see that over the next five years, there would be three more funerals for me to plan, three more eulogies to prepare and deliver.

The many tasks associated with death. Like choosing the clothes my father would be buried in. My mother asked me to do it. She said she couldn't face it – I wasn't sure I could either, but someone had to and that someone was me. It felt inappropriate fossicking in my father's wardrobe, so I pretended I was packing to send him off on a business trip. A short trip, only one night, but very important and he had to look his best. I selected a dark blue suit and crisp pale blue shirt, folding them neatly into the carry case. Fingering his impressive assortment of ties, I chose a blue and red striped silk one then sat on the bed and sobbed. There was something so personal about selecting his tie and it broke me. However much I tried to pretend, I knew my father's last business trip was destination – Heaven, and the important appointment was with his Maker.

The funeral.

My mother went to church most Sundays. My father attended at Christmas and Easter. Encouraging him to go more regularly, my mother once said, "Twice a year isn't enough. Father David doesn't know you. He won't bury you when you die!"

My father laughed and said, "Oh yes he will. You are there every week – he knows you."

And he was right. A beautiful day in early March, still redolent of summer but with the slightest hint of autumn crispness in the breeze. The packed church and Father David conducting the service with poise and grace for his faithful parishioner sitting heart-broken but dry eyed in the front pew, her little granddaughters on either side of her. Amelia insisted on wearing her sparkly sandals and the sight of her skinny little feet encased in shiny sequins was almost too much for me.

The most modest and unassuming of men, how surprised my father would have been at the size of the congregation. Clutching the podium ready to begin my eulogy, I looked across at the crowd and could hear him say, "All these people here! Don't they have anything better to do today?"

Afterwards we stood by the newly dug grave, surrounded by masses of flowers and wreaths. My mother scattered soil from their garden into the grave and I read Mary Frye's poem – *Do Not Stand at My Grave and Weep.*

I had always loved this poem. Loved the thought of living on in diamond snow, ripening grain, the circling flight of quiet birds. Now it was comforting to reassure everyone that my father was not here. Not in this sleek, small – I never realised coffins were so small! – polished casket. He was somewhere else. At that point, I wasn't as strong in my faith as I am now to be certain of exactly where he was. But I knew it was somewhere that – for the moment at least – was not accessible to us.

Hungarian funerals are usually conducted without music and my mother said she didn't want hymns during the service. This made sense – unless we sang Silent Night or the Halleluiah Chorus, none of the usual hymns would have been meaningful to my twice a year church-going father. But it was unthinkable not to include some music – such an important part of my father's life. The service began with Beethoven's Pastoral Symphony and ended with the Adagio in G Minor by Albinoni, two of his favourite classical pieces. And at the graveside, as my mother had requested, Autumn Leaves.

Made famous in the 1950s by Nat King Cole, my father always considered this "their" song. Countless times, nearing the end of a red wine fuelled Hungarian get-together, my father serenaded my mother with it, while I hid in the bathroom, pretending I wasn't related to him.

Once cringingly sentimental, the words seemed prophetic now.

In the weeks that followed, I learned many things. I learned that bravery can consist of something as ordinary as waking up in the morning in the bed you had shared with your husband for many years and realising, as if for the first time, he was not beside you and never would be again. Then getting out of bed and making yourself face the day.

I learned that my father and the man who owned the general store on the corner bonded long ago through a shared love of European soccer and Cadbury's Roasted Almond Dark Chocolate. Going in to buy milk soon after Dad's death, I was confronted by an emotional, elderly Italian who hugged me and insisted on presenting me with a large block, saying, "One in a million, your papa! One in a million!"

And perhaps most importantly, I learned that grief is not linear. It did not begin the day my father died, progress neatly through a stretch of time, then fade gently away. Grief is tidal – ebbing and flowing. Seeming sometimes to retreat completely and then, when I least expected it, rush violently back at me and sweep me under in a tsunami of grief. Unless you have been there, it's difficult to comprehend that one year or many later, these feelings can be just as devastating as at the very beginning. Which explains the otherwise kind lady's expression of surprise at my sadness. "But hasn't he been dead for six months?"

Correct. Also – irrelevant.

Grief coupled with an overwhelming sense of loss.

When your partner commits adultery and then up and leaves, you lose not just that person and your future with them. The betrayal also steals your past, dimming, somehow diminishing even the memory of the happiest times you shared. Or so I've been reliably informed.

Losing my father felt the same. Death had not only taken him and the future I now would not have with him. I had also lost his past. All those memories that he had not yet shared with me. And the minute details of the ones he had. Details that suddenly seemed vitally important. The many things I suddenly needed to ask him but now could not.

Your parents' sitting room in the house in Győr? Remember – you described the painting hanging there and how much you loved it. Frolicking horses, a hay cart and storks nesting on a thatched roof. The painting that had to be sold to buy food in 1943? Were the walls of the room cream? Or pale green? I think it was one or the other- you told me once but now, I can't remember exactly which. And I must know. I really want to know. For some reason I can't even begin to explain, I feel a great need at this moment to picture you as a little boy in that room, but I can't unless I know the colour.

The name of your fourth-grade teacher – the one who kept falling asleep in class? He used to wake up suddenly and throw chalk at any boy he caught laughing. What was his name again? You told me his name once, but I wasn't listening. I was doing something else and his name didn't matter then. But now it is important. It is part of your past. I need to have your past now, in all its wonderful minutiae. Now that I don't have your future. Don't have you.

If it was painful for me, it was a hundred times more so for my mother. I know in the days immediately following the funeral – when the flowers began to wilt and she could no longer pretend it was all a very bad dream – she was not sure she actually could live without my father. And not at all sure she really wanted to.

But the same steely strength that enabled her to leave her homeland, her family, all her friends and start afresh with only a suitcase full of possessions reasserted itself. She decided she owed it to my father to keep on keeping on. She knew he would want her to put aside her grief and if not exactly rebuild her life

– without him that would not be possible – build a new life for herself in its place.

There were things she still needed to do, she decided. Like being here for her grand-daughters, watching them grow up, showering them with affection and chocolate and making sure they never forgot the man who had loved them so very much. Their Otto-Papa – the dear special name Amelia bestowed on him when she was learning to talk and which he had been so proud of.

And there were things she promised herself she would not do. Cry. Be dependent on her children. Be a burden to her friends. She was determined to just take each day as it came and not give way to despair – especially during the long sleepless nights. Her days continued to be filled with company, but she dreaded the nights.

I visited her at least twice a week in the first few months and it was not unusual to arrive and find a bunch of obviously home-grown flowers left on her front doorstep. Or a magazine, 'I thought you might enjoy reading this story', written on a yellow post-it-note slipped inside. Or a plate of cake or biscuits – never as delicious as the ones my mother made – but baked and delivered with love.

My parents had lived in this cul-de-sac for over 40 years and some of their neighbours almost as long and these gifts were usually from people I knew well. But at times, people I had never even heard of exhibited random acts of kindness, so out of keeping with our apparently increasingly disconnected, selfish world.

One day, I arrived to be greeted by the scent of newly mown grass and my mother telling me, "Harry has been over and done the front lawn."

Harry? Not a neighbour, not a friend. Just a local man – owner of a gardening business, living three streets away. His wife knew my mother from church and sent him over.

And of course, the Hungarians kept in constant touch, visiting often and telephoning almost every night. If I didn't know them so well, I would have thought they had organised some sort of roster but that wasn't how they did things. They just knew their dear friend needed them and they responded.

More than anything, they wanted to show my mother how much they loved her, loved my father and always would. And while yes, 'Food is Love,' this part was tricky – owing to the unwritten but unbreakable rule that you never, ever, ever take something edible to a Hungarian woman's home. Not a meal, a cake, biscuits, nothing that hints, be it ever so mildly, that she is unable to cook for herself.

Personally, I think it's a dumb tradition. There are times of crisis in life when food – cooked by someone else – is *exactly* what you need. Hungarian women of my mother's generation didn't agree, and she would have been shocked and not a little offended to be presented with the 'you probably don't want to cook right now so I've made you a casserole' offering so beloved of Australians. A true Magyar housewife had to be laid up with two broken arms and at least one broken leg plus a fractured ankle not to want to cook. Implying otherwise was simply not on.

However, inviting someone over and loving them up by feeding them in your own home – that was not only acceptable. It was mandatory.

My mother was inundated with invitations for dinner, lunch, breakfast, which at first, she was able to decline, saying that she just didn't feel up to going out. Finally, after many weeks she forced herself to accept and prepared to drive from Freshwater on the northern beaches to the dinner party in Sydney's eastern suburbs. In Hungary, a trip of around 45km each way may not actually necessitate you taking your passport to facilitate crossing national boarders, but a packed lunch and a change of underwear is considered prudent.

In the 50-plus years since they arrived in Australia, my parents had become accustomed to travelling long distances. After all, this was the couple who in their 60s set off for eight months in a campervan and made their merry way from Sydney to Melbourne, Adelaide, then across the desert to Alice Springs. Then back again via the coast roads, while their less adventurous adult children engaged in violent eye rolling and indignant exclamations of, "Are you kidding me?!" as postcards arrived from Coober Pedi, Broken Hill and other far flung destinations.

Even when they were not annoying their children in this way, they thought nothing of heading off to Bilpin in the Blue Mountains so my mother could buy Pink Lady apples from her favourite orchard.

Unlike some immigrant groups, when initially settling in our capital cities, Hungarians did not congregate in particular suburbs. They spread themselves around. My parents regularly visited friends as far away as Hurstville, Parramatta, Palm Beach, Burwood, Rose Bay, Connells Point and Wahroonga. Driving to a dinner party anywhere in Sydney was not an issue for them.

But – and this was the part that was now causing my poor mother many hours of anxiety – from the time my father so proudly purchased his first car in 1962, he had been Designated Driver. My mother felt much more comfortable as chief navigator, hander out of peppermints, finder of classical music radio stations and occasionally – though in my father's opinion, far too frequently – dispenser of gentle driving advice along the lines of, "Darling, I know 72km per hour is pretty close to 60km but maybe not close enough?"

Despite his lead foot, my dad was an excellent driver. When it was time for my mother to learn to drive after my brother was born, my mother assumed that he would prove to be an excellent teacher. She was wrong. My dad had been blessed with many gifts, but Natural Born Teacher was not on the list. He was too exacting and impatient, something I quickly discovered during his – fortunately short-lived – attempt to improve my piano technique when I was about twelve. Although quickly abandoned, my mother could not have been unaware of the tension behind the closed door of the sitting room where discordant notes and exasperated exclamations battled for supremacy.

Not being dependent on natural talent but a simple set of skills and the ability to keep to the road, teaching your wife to drive was in another category entirely. Or so I assumed my poor deluded parents believed. The first few driving lessons ended in tears on her part, barely concealed frustration on his but she was determined to keep going. The fact that at this point, family finances would be stretched to afford driving lessons may have had something to do with it.

On the fourth lesson, it all unravelled quite spectacularly. Something to do with not enough choke, too much clutch, unacceptable kangaroo-hopping (was that even a thing?). My mother ended up sitting behind the wheel, stalled in a line of traffic. Furious drivers all around her and a fuming husband next to her. My father shouted at her. She shouted back. Things got decidedly heated. Finally, totally fed up, my mother leapt out of the car and stormed off home on foot, leaving my father in the passenger seat surrounded by open-mouthed occupants of other cars.

Fortunately, it was only a short walk home. Unfortunately, as my mother got to the front gate, she realised she was still holding the car key, which in her agitation, she had yanked from the ignition.

My father arrived on foot some time later and... well, it might be best to leave it there.

But that was a long time ago. They stayed married and my mother became a competent driver, thanks to Eddie's Driving School, Manly Branch.

Now many years later, she set off alone on this, her first solo excursion as a widow. She kept telling herself she knew the route well – they were old friends whose house she and my father had been to innumerable times. How difficult could it be?

All went well until she got over – or rather – under the harbour, when like many people unaccustomed to driving through Sydney's Harbour Tunnel, she ended up in the wrong lane. She kept going, hoping it would sort of fix itself and the familiar streets of Rushcutters Bay miraculously reveal themselves. They didn't. She became more and more lost. Eventually after what seemed like several hours but was probably no more than 20 minutes, she ended up in the back streets of Redfern. And the back streets of Redfern were not then, and I hazard a guess probably never will be, a haven for the faint hearted. Especially those who have no idea where they are.

In these pre-sat nav days, she fumbled in the glove-box for the street directory and in a feat of navigational excellence (something I could never hope to emulate) worked out not only where she was but how she could get to where she needed to be. Had in fact needed to be over half an hour ago, to be totally accurate.

It was a simple matter of taking the second left, then third right, second right and then crossing South Dowling Street. But first, she had to make her way out of this narrow one-way street that somehow – she had no idea how – she had ended up in. In her agitated state, reversing was not an option, so she decided to turn the car around. Misjudging the width of the car or the width of the street or some pesky combination of both, she ended up wedged.

Heaven only knows what she would have done next but then – the Police arrived.

My dad sent them. In answer to her frantic prayers. Or so to her dying day my mother believed. In which case, these law enforcement officers didn't have far to travel on their mission of mercy. The street backed onto Police Headquarters and they used it to park their cars while on shift.

Anyway, the police –'two absolutely delightful blond young men' – not only helped her unwedge her car but instructed her to drive behind them while they escorted her onto the correct road.

Arriving almost an hour late to the dinner, she was greeted as a heroine by the other guests. To this day, the story of her Police Escort is told at Hungarian gatherings, usually prefaced by the joke one of my father's wittiest friends made up on the night:

What is the difference between police in Australia in 2007 and police in Hungary in 1957?

In Australia – if they find you lost behind the police station, the police drive you home.

In socialist Hungary – if they find you lost behind the police station, the police beat you to a pulp then steal your shoes.

Having recovered from this adventure, my mother found getting home much easier, as is so often the case and the next morning, woke up exhilarated and the closest to joy she had felt since my father's death.

Just like she had so often done in the past, that afternoon she decided to bake. With skill borne of long experience, she quickly assembled all the ingredients and then masterfully mixed and beat and smoothed until a magnificent chocolate cake sat shimmering in the oven, rising slowly and symmetrically. She had forgotten how much she enjoyed doing this and soon the indescribable aroma of cake filled the kitchen. When the cake was ready and cooling on the bench, she set to work again. She would cut it into four layers, filling them with hazelnut cream, topped with a glossy ganache.

My father's favourite.

So immersed was she in working her culinary arts, for a few precious minutes she actually forgot he was dead. Spreading the rich cream on the cake, she listened with half an ear for the sound of his footsteps in the garage. Soon, he would come in from the garden. She would make him a cup of tea to drink with the cake. He would look at the piece she cut him and protest, like he always did, "That's far too big!" before eating it all, scraping his fork along the bottom of the plate to capture the last of the cream.

Then she remembered. Silence. No footsteps outside or the opening of the door. He was not coming in. He would not be with her again. Never again.

Defeated at last, she sat down at the table, put her head into her hands and wept.

Otto attacking the cake on his 70th birthday.
The writing on the cake reads:
God grant you a long life.
Tragically - He didn't.

CHAPTER 14
Going Home

A treatment is not a cure. Dr N explained this very carefully to us right at the beginning and we assured him we understood. But as the months went by and my mother's strength and vitality returned, we chose to forget. Chose to believe that the Miracle Pills (as my mother insisted on calling them) had indeed cured her. We were wrong. All they did – and for this I remain eternally grateful – was temporarily halt the progression of the metastatic lung cancer cells invading her bones and liver while they made their way to her brain. Then, as suddenly as the pills started working, they stopped. Within a few days, my mother was pale, weak, wracked with nausea.

Despite how unwell she felt, she remained committed to her day to day routine. To do otherwise was to surrender. And the word surrender – not ever and especially not now – wasn't part of her vocabulary. She continued to fight, determined to beat 'This terrible thing'. Right at the start, she christened her cancer, 'This terrible thing'. By distancing herself from her disease and setting it apart from her, she hoped to vanquish it.

"I'm only in my mid-seventies," she reminded me more than once. "Women in my family always live into their nineties and I'm not leaving yet!" At that time, she called it leaving. She would not say dying until the very end.

Although our monthly appointment wasn't for another three weeks, I suggested we go see Dr N urgently, but she refused. "He is a very busy man and doesn't need us disturbing him. We will go when I have my next appointment," she declared stubbornly. "Anyway, I might feel better by then." She didn't. She felt worse. As soon as Dr N saw her, he knew. Watching his face, the expression in his kind brown eyes, I knew too. This miracle had run its course.

Although it was clearly no longer having any affect, Dr N agreed to increase her medication to one and a half Miracle Pills a day and then spent precious minutes showing us how to divide the little white discs as precisely as possible. He also enthusiastically endorsed my mother's suggestion about taking extra vitamins. When the treatment had first kicked in, she regained her energy almost overnight but her usually robust appetite remained sluggish. On her trip back to Hungary twelve months ago, a friend recommended a very special vitamin supplement. Having beaten breast cancer not long before, the friend waxed lyrical over these tablets (large, pale green, to be chewed and never swallowed whole) but warned that they were incredibly hard to come by. Which obviously proved how good they were, according to her.

My mother was keen to try them. The Hungary-based Tom-Toms (every bit as efficient as the Sydney-based ones) immediately went into overdrive. By the time she returned home, she had eight bottles in her possession. The tablets did seem to help and when she ran out, I spent hours on the internet sourcing more. Directly from Switzerland, this batch was so eye-wateringly expensive it might have been cheaper to contact her Hungarian buddy, ask her to pull together the same team, reimburse them twice the cost, then fly to Hungary to collect them myself. Premium Economy.

But by the time we saw Dr N, although my mother was diligently chewing the tablets three times a day, it was about the only thing she was chewing and most of the weight she regained during her remission had dropped off. Dr N encouraged her to increase the dose to four tablets daily. When my mother asked him – with a flash of her old humour – if she was permitted to have a glass of red wine to wash them down at night, the dear man smiled. "Of course. Even two glasses if you enjoy it. But only if it's a really good vintage."

When we left his surgery, my mother was upbeat, chatting about the holiday season just around the corner. I tried hard to enter into the spirt and failed. One look at her grey skin and gaunt frame told me exactly how things stood.

By the time Christmas arrived, my mother was extremely unwell, but she battled on. She even insisted we celebrate Christmas Eve at her place, while she prepared the usual gargantuan feast. I protested when she first mentioned it, suggesting we transfer the festivities to our home where I could do most of the cooking. This break from tradition was met with an icy glare and adamant refusal. "No!" she said, wagging her index finger at me to drive the point home. "No! "We are having Christmas here. And I'm cooking. Like always." So, we had no choice but to assemble as we had every other year. Celebrating Christ's arrival while we silently bore witness to my mother's imminent departure.

December 24th was a typically steamy summer day. According to custom, we sat upstairs before dinner to take advantage of the sea breeze. The air shimmered with humidity and ocean spray, an impressive assortment of nibbles was laid out on the coffee table and enticing aromas drifted up from the kitchen. My mother had even maintained my dad's rather questionable musical offerings. In the background, Bing Crosby's gentle crooning about sleighbells and falling snow competed incongruously with Sydney's heatwave. The adults guzzled champagne and far too many cheese sticks and chili nuts. My daughter and niece giggled together on the couch next to my mother who made sure they had a vast selection of chocolate and other treats within easy reach in case they felt peckish. We all fell over ourselves pretending that everything was as it had been for so many happy years.

Eventually I found it unbearable and escaped downstairs into the kitchen to check on the food. I stood by the breakfast bar and out of sheer force of habit, nibbled on tiny pieces of honey crusted ham. As much a tradition as Bing warbling and the guests eating far too much, every year while everyone else drank and chatted upstairs, I crept into the kitchen and plundered the ham, baked earlier in the day by my unsuspecting mother and left to cool.

For as long as I could remember, the ham was the centrepiece of our feast. Without fail, she managed to prepare it so that the thick shiny crust was crisp and golden, tasting sweet, salty, tantalisingly piquant from the brown sugar, mustard and Guinness glaze she painstakingly massaged into it. Underneath this ambrosial covering, the meat itself was moist, juicy and meltingly tender. It was totally irresistible. Every 24th December, I happily laid my cholesterol count on the altar of gluttony and tucked in. It was my secret vice. Although not completely secret.

Many years ago, I had been acutely embarrassed when my father suddenly appeared in the kitchen while I was in mid-gorge. I almost choked on my mouthful. But there was no need to concoct some story along the lines of 'just making sure the ham was cooked…'

As if I did not exist, my father headed for the drinks' cupboard. To reach this, he actually had to walk behind me, which he did, all the while pretending I wasn't in the room. So, I pretended he wasn't in the room either. He poured himself a sizeable (and usually forbidden) shot of whisky. Knocking it back neatly, and with still not a word exchanged between us, he turned on his heal and headed back upstairs to re-join the others. The ham and I stayed behind, pondering, "Who was that man?"

Even though we never spoke of this encounter – or indeed during it – every subsequent Christmas my father and I met in the kitchen and played at being invisible. It became as much a part of the evening as the sparklers on the tree or the table groaning with food. Since his death four years before, I missed my partner in crime and never more so than right now. I would have given anything for him to walk in again, so we could begin our charade. To have things the way they had been when he was alive. The house filled with life and laughter, my father in his element playing host and my mother bustling around in her big apron, in full glorious flight as she presided over the festivities. Instead, I was floundering around like a shipwreck-survivor, clinging desperately to tradition, watching my precious world disintegrated before my eyes.

Somehow, we got through that Christmas. And the New Year.

In February, Amelia started high school – a 12-year-old beauty with olive skin, honey coloured hair and my father's grey-blue eyes. She adored her grandmother and even now willingly set aside the cool tweenager persona she normally cultivated to spend many weekends and most of every school holiday with 'Denma'. Remembering her confusion and pain at my father's unexpected death, I tried to prepare her for this new tragedy. She was no longer the round-faced seven year-old who had been so indignant at Otto-Papa's passing, "He can't be dead! I love him!" she cried when first told the news, angry that her love had not tethered him to life. But Amelia faced this new tragedy bravely while I felt helpless at not being able to ease her pain.

How was I facing it? I wondered on those long nights when I woke at 3am, exhausted yet unable to sleep from the jumble of thoughts colliding inside my brain. How was I facing it? And how would I be able to face the future without my mother?

When I was young, we had not been close. My grandmother had been the most important person in my life then. After her suddenly death when I was 18, I muddled through on my own. Looking back now, I can see that my mother had always been there for me – all I needed to do was reach out. I didn't. That was my loss. And hers.

But once Amelia was born, my relationship with both my parents blossomed. They loved her so intensely – this tiny scrap of humanity I had finally, miraculously, managed to produce after many painful years of infertility. It would be fair to say that the happiest day of their lives was when Amelia was born, followed five years later when my niece made her appearance. They launched themselves into grand-parenting head first and I could not have survived those bewildering sleep-deprived early years without them.

As Amelia grew, starting to walk and talk, their devotion grew with her. She had her own room at their place and considered it her second home. I once joked to a friend that whenever I went to collect my daughter, I was afraid I would need a court order to regain custody from my parents. Or at least reasonable access. But it was such a blessing for all of us.

Watching them interact with Amelia was a revelation to me. My father – never the most patient of men – sat with her on the floor for hours, (this from a man who refused to sit on an armchair if he considered it too low!) helping her play with blocks – endlessly piling them up, just to watch her squeal with laughter as she smashed them down. He took her for strolls along the beach. My father's loathing of sand was legendary and when I found out he removed his shoes and socks to walk on the beach with her, I knew she held his heart firmly in her tiny toddler hands.

Although I'm sure he had harboured a secret hope that at long last, here was the family's musical prodigy of the next generation, he even forgave Amelia her lack of musical talent. When it became clear that she had not inherited the legendary Lang perfect ear/beautiful singing voice, his only comment was, "It doesn't matter. She will be good at lots of other things." My mother and I looked at each other in amazement.

Despite no longer having her debut at the Sydney Opera House Young Performers Concert to look forward to in a few years' time, he continued to encourage her musical efforts. Dad's arthritis made playing more complex pieces acutely painful, but they loved the nursery rhymes and little songs they performed together. Perched next to him while he picked out simple tunes on the piano, concentration oozing from every pore, Amelia waited until he gave her the signal to hit middle C, which she did with great energy and about 90% accuracy.

Occasionally they gave Proper Concerts. This consisted of my father performing a slightly longer, more elaborate piece with Amelia who had been promoted to playing several notes in succession. Even my mother was roped in. Wide eyed with terror but determined not to disappoint her fellow performers, my mother stood clutching the shiny new triangle my father had purchased from the local music store. On cue, she struck her instrument as many times as instructed, while Amelia loudly bashed out her assigned notes. The only time I witness this performance, I laughed so hard it hurt. You know the kind of laughter that leaves you doubled up, grasping for breath, tears running down your cheeks? That kind.

When not honing her percussion skills, my mother looked after Amelia tenderly and selflessly, every bit as smitten as my father. At night, she tucked her up in bed and told her stories about her own childhood. Magical tales where all the animals in the village could talk, simple daily tasks became the stuff of great adventure and the grinding privation of the war years turned into comedy. When not regaling her spellbound granddaughter with stories about Denma's Olden Days, my mother spent hours preparing Amelia's favourite meals and teaching her basic cooking skills. Without doubt, Denma and Otto-Papa were Amelia's favourite people. How could I not love them too?

My mother became my confidant. My friend. Her empathy was soothing, her advice always practical and well-considered, her cakes delicious and I always left her feeling I was not going to be knocked unconscious by the curve balls life threw at me.

Over the past few years, the curve balls had come thick and fast. Beginning with my father's death, several important aspects of my life unravelled in quick succession. Things I thought were secure, had blithely taken for granted, came tumbling down. A deeply painful time but while I struggled to come to grips with it, my mother's support was unfailing. Whatever happened, however awful, however heartbreaking, I knew I did not have to face it alone. Even if I couldn't share all the details of what was going on for me, she always had my back – supporting, enabling, loving me. She believed I would get through it and her confidence helped me believe I could too.

During this time, another relationship began to have immense and profound meaning for me – my relationship with God. As my life spiralled downhill, God entered in and made my struggles bearable. He gave my pain context and meaning. He blessed me with hope and strengthened my faith.

"What does it profit a man to gain the whole world and lose his immortal soul?" Christ asks His disciples. For me it happened in reverse. While there were times – many times – when I felt I had lost a big chunk of my whole world, through those losses I gained my immortal soul. My relationship with God became strong, alive, a source of immense consolation. Or more accurately, the relationship became real. I had grown up a believer, a Catholic girl who tried to be 'good' and regularly fell far short of the mark. Previously, my only interaction with the Almighty had been through the church. At its best, this interaction was comforting but never particularly close. Most of the time however, it oscillated between distant and impersonal or cold and remote. Now, I developed a truly personal relationship directly with God. No middlemen to cloud or obscure or confuse. While church remained the setting where God and I could meet, these days I met Him daily, hourly, minute by minute as I journeyed through this thing called Life.

But that is a whole other story. And right now, I'm telling this one.

Suffice to say, my newfound faith – personal, intimate, immensely precious – gave me the strength to watch my mother take her final steps through the Valley of the Shadow of Death. God also gave me the wisdom and the strength to help her take them. It requires great courage to face death but as I was discovering, it also requires courage to speak about it. This courage, if coupled with strong faith, makes the conversation profound and of real meaning.

Australians don't do this well while the English try not to do it at all. Even the Hungarians – much given to loud breast-beating, totally in-your-face emoting about most things can cry, mourn, accept death and continue to talk lovingly and long about the deceased but not actually talk about mortality with the one who is dying. Yet now, what my poor mother needed most was to talk about it. She was desperate for someone to say the words she needed to hear and to hear – really hear – the words she needed to say.

At the very time I was discovering how close God could be to me if I cared to seek Him, losing my father so tragically had greatly weakened my mother's belief in the Almighty. Feeling betrayed and abandoned, she began to shut Him out. She simply could not understand how God – whom she had loved and tried to serve all her life, albeit from a respectful Catholic-church infused distance – could have let something so terrible happen. She confided to me that in the first few weeks after dad's death, much to her surprise and shame, she often found herself yelling at her Maker. She couldn't help herself. Unable to pray, she could only admonish and demand, "How could You? Why did You?"

She continued attending Mass most Sundays. But increasingly, it was like Dr N upping her dose on that last visit. Those who mattered most knew it was window dressing.

Finding out she had cancer was the final nail in the coffin of her old fashioned, conservative, Hungarian convent-girl belief in God. This time, He really had let her down – bigtime. She turned her back on Him. For good measure, she banged the door in His face and hung up the Do Not Disturb sign. Immediately after her diagnosis when she spent a few days in hospital, one of the elderly Sisters visited her, prompted by the Catholic notation on her Admissions Record. My mother politely but firmly told her to push off. "If you have come to talk to me about God, please don't bother. He and I are not friends right now." It was the one and only time in her life when she spoke confrontationally to a nun.

She survived for only nine weeks after that last excruciating Christmas. Nine terrible weeks when I watched her disappearing day by day. And through it all, she kept trying so hard to pretend. Until the day came when she stopped pretending.

She told me she had asked all her friends not to visit her any more. I was on the verge of making some inane remark about waiting until she was better before having visitors. But then I didn't. It was time for me to speak the truth. And it was time to give her the space to speak it.

I believe it was grace – the miraculous, unmerited love of God – that gave me the courage to ask, "Why don't you want to see them?"

We looked at each other. My mother had never been one for tears but now they glistened in her eyes.

"I don't want them to see me like this. I hate what I have become. Sick. Weak. I want them to remember me as I was.

"I'm dying – it won't be long now.

"Promise me," she took my hand. "Promise me – that I can stay at home for as long as possible."

I desperately wanted to tell her not to be silly. Tell her she would get better. Tell her anything to end this conversation. But she was being so brave now, speaking the unspeakable. The only way to honour her bravery was to be brave myself.

"I promise. I promise I will do everything I can to make sure you remain at home until the end."

Then bursting into tears, I clung to her seeking comfort. As always, she had comfort to give me.

After that, death was no longer taboo. We spoke of it often – death and the future in which she would no longer play her part.

Ever organised and practical, she asked me to look after Amelia and my niece Angie. And my brother. My husband, my stepchildren, my uncle, her beloved 98-year-old German neighbour, and what seemed like half the Hungarian community.

'And who is going to look after me?' I wondered sadly as she carefully committed each one into my care. 'Who is going to look after my mangled, battered heart?'

But I didn't burden her with this. My mother was leaving me a loving, demanding, heavy legacy. And if she believed I was strong enough to bear it; I would have to be.

To my great joy and relief, during these last weeks, she mended her relationship with God.

"I miss your father so much. I was furious with God when He took my Otto," she admitted to me one day.

"But I've made my peace with Him. I think I understand now, not why Otto died so young but why He left me here for five years. To finish what I had still had to do. And to give you the time you needed to grow strong. You will take over from me. You will look after everyone when I'm gone.

"Now I'm going to be with my darling. I wanted to stay so much – to watch our precious little girls grow up. But I accept now that I won't, and I've made my peace with that too. I'm ready now."

The last time my mother cooked for us was the day before my birthday when she insisted we all go over to celebrate. Barely able to stand, she made profiteroles – always my favourite birthday treat. They were perfectly crisp, the filling deliciously light and not too sweet. She even drank a half glass of champagne to toast the event.

The next morning, my brother phoned as soon as I arrived at work. While my colleagues gathered to wish me happy birthday, I ran to my car and sped over to her place. When I arrived, it was exactly as John had said – my mother was unable to get out of bed, confused and disoriented. Before leaving the office, I phoned Dr N. He told me to take her to hospital – where she could be cared for while I organised nursing care. Then she would come home, just as I had promised. I helped her get up, shower, dress and then drove her to hospital, where Dr N – bless him! – had already arranged her admission.

As we sat in Emergency, waiting for the room to be ready for her, she rallied. For the next half hour, we chatted about inconsequential things.

Suddenly she turned to me and said, "I've had such a good, happy life. Your father. You and your brother. Then my beautiful little girls. Many friends and everything I could ever want. I've been so blessed."

I will carry the memory of our last conversation forever. We went on to speak of love, of forgiveness, of God's mercy and our belief in the life to come. All the things we had never been able to say to one another before but now were gifted not only with the opportunity but with the words we needed.

We sat holding hands. Then she said she was hungry. When I returned with a sandwich – the only thing I could find in the half-closed canteen – she ate it happily. It was the ultimate irony. This generous, talented preparer of hundreds, thousands of delicious meals, who understood and appreciated food more than anyone I've ever met, had a tomato and cheese sandwich for her last meal. And she said it was delicious.

It happened very quickly after that. While they settled her into her room, I noticed the corner of her mouth was drooping. I mentioned it to the nurse, but she said she was probably just tired and needed to rest. My mother insisted I leave – she was fine and would see me in the morning. Foraging in her wallet for her Medicare card, I found my father's photo. I handed it to her.

Smiling at me, she raised the photo to her lips and kissed it. Then closed her eyes and fell asleep.

She had a massive stroke that night and never regained consciousness.

I spent the next three days sitting by my mother's bedside, waiting for her to die. I sensed we were not going to receive a miraculous healing – it was time to let her go. I knew it was what my mother wanted – she was ready. I kept replaying our final conversation, grateful that we had been given that last precious time together. She knew she was leaving, knew where she was going and welcomed it. She had no regrets. Just gratitude and a true awareness of all she had been blessed with. And because of our honesty with each other as she approached the end, I had no regrets either. My grief was not tarnished by thoughts of what I wish we had been able to say to each other. Everything we needed to say had been said. All that was left was love. Another blessing among the many.

They had put her into a lovely sunny room with big windows. If I stood by her bed and looked out, I could see the city's tall buildings silhouetted against the sky and watch the spectacular sunsets. Red and gold light as the burning sun plunged below the horizon. My mother loved welcoming the day from her balcony at home – the sun coming up out of the ocean in a glorious spectacle every morning. Sunrises herald beginnings. These sunsets, every bit as beautiful, heralded the final goodbye in this life.

Although I accepted what was happening, indeed, was grateful for it, there were still times during my long vigil when it just did not seem real to me. Who is this shrunken motionless woman in the bed, her breath coming in shallow waves? I found myself wondering. It could not be my mother. My mother was dynamic, constantly on the go. And she was pretty. Even in her

70s, her wavy hair was thick and lustrous. Unlike this emaciated old woman with her dull hair and grey, lifeless clammy skin.

Before being stricken with cancer, my mother had never been sick. Her only connection to illness was to care for people when they were. Her famous chicken soup – fragrant, delicious, magical – and her practical, loving care had restored many to health. The helpless dying woman could not possibly be my mother. Occasionally I found myself staring at the closed door, willing it to open to reveal my mother. Healthy and vigorous, she would rush in, carrying a big bunch of flowers and a huge thermos of soup. And when she arrived, I could go home. She would take over, nurse this poor woman and make her well again. But however much I longed for her, she did not come. The silence remained unbroken except for the shallow rasping sound that filled the room.

Every night I went home to sleep for a few hours only after extracting the solemn promise from the nursing staff that they would call me if I was needed. My brother came several times every day, offered to stay and was relieved when I told him to go. I didn't resent that. We all had to cope in our own way. I knew I needed to be here and he knew he did not.

The days were long, punctuated by my brother's visits and frequent offers of cups of tea from the dedicated staff. No-one else came. My mother's friends respected my wish that they not visit. Loving her as they did, they understood when I explained that – just as mum had not wanted them to see her when she was so ill – she would not want anyone to see her as she lay dying. But while they did not come here, they spent hours at each other's homes, crying, reminiscing, eating. And twice each day I called one or other of them and reported in. There was never anything new to tell them so the calls were mercifully short and excruciatingly painful.

Some of the time, I sat in the comfortable chair the nurses had given me and pretended to read – the daily paper or the book I'd brought with me. Every lunchtime, I forced myself to go down to the café and get myself something to eat. One day, I chanced upon a Poppy Seed and Orange Friand. After a mouthful I pushed it aside and heard my mother say very clearly, "Too dry. Baked about three minutes too long."

But mostly I just sat looking out of the window, losing myself in memories. Leafing through them carefully. Holding as firmly as I could to those days where illness and death had not yet staked their claim, I found myself smiling through my tears.

My favourite memories centred around our weekender in Bowral, which we bought just before Amelia was born. My parents loved this part of the world as much as we did. Mum was thrilled to finally have a big fertile plot to work her magic on. She was in her element in that acre of rich red soil – planting a vegetable garden (much to the delight of the many possums), pruning the rose bushes and mercilessly bossing the rest of us around. My husband and I didn't have a clue about gardening, so we were grateful for her benevolent dictatorship. My father was used to acting as the hired help. Soon the garden was blooming.

My parents often went down during the week and we joined them on Friday for the weekend. It was the ultimate Win/Win. My husband and I got to SLEEP IN – a rare treat when Amelia tended to wake up at 5.30 every morning. Standing in her cot, with a huge toothless grin, loudly yelling, "Come now, Denma!" as Denma sprinted down the hallway, her dressing gown flapping behind her. A welcome change from the usual louds calls for Mumma. Everyone benefited – Amelia got to spend more time with her favourite people and my parents were allowed 24/7 access to their adored grand-daughter.

Before Amelia went to pre-school and I returned to part-time work, the two of us always drove down to Bowral together. Loading up the car with Bananas in Pyjamas CD, snacks and her pink sippie cup, we usually headed off early on Friday morning, leaving Stuart to follow by train in the evening. My parents would already be in situ. "To get the house ready," my mother always insisted, but in truth so as not to miss a second of their cherished grand-daughter's company.

Because the traffic was always so unpredictable, I would overestimate how long it would take us and we usually got to the house at least half an hour before my ETA. Had we been on time, I would have found both my parents loitering by the front gate, pretending to garden as they kept watch for our car. On one occasion, we arrived especially early. Through the big glass doors, I could see them still eating their breakfast in the dining room. But the moment they heard the crunch of the wheels on the gravel, propelled like bullets shot from a double barrel shotgun, they leapt to their feet and raced to the back door. As I stopped the car, I was greeted by the hilarious spectacle of my mother and father trying to push and jostle each other out of the way. The winner got to open the passenger door and extract Amelia, so as you can imagine, the stakes were high.

I watched while they got wedged in the doorway in an absurd spectacle of arms and legs and shouty Hungarian. I laughed, and Amelia – delighted to be reunited with her grandparents – waved her little plump arms around. "Huwwy up! Huwwy up!" she yelled encouragingly. As if they needed to be told.

While the drama in the hospital was unfolding, Amelia was away on a school camp. She knew her grandmother was very ill but not that we had come to the end. I prayed about a lot of things during those days but my most fervent prayer was that my mother would die before Amelia returned home. I wanted to spare her the heartbreak of waiting, even if I couldn't spare her the agony of loss. And in what I believe was her final gift to her grand-daughter, my mother died the day before Amelia returned. I wasn't there with her either – and I think it was how she wanted it. She slipped away quietly while I was walking back to her room.

I sat with her and waited for my brother to arrive. The room felt empty. I was alone. The body on the bed no longer contained my mother; like a coat she now did not need, she had taken it off. The essence of who she had been – her soul – was no longer here. She had left us to be reunited with my father. It is not wishful thinking that makes me write this or a fervent desire that there is life after death. I truly believe it. Sitting with my mother immediately after she died – amid the stillness – and there is no other word for it – grace that infused the room – confirmed to me as nothing has before or since, the miracle, the mystery of life and death. And the existence of a loving God.

In those happy years before dad died, as every boisterous Hungarian dinner party drew to its song and wine-fuelled close, I remembered how my mother would go in search of my father. Finally locating him in a corner with his buddies, she would go up to him, take his hand and say, *"Gyere drágám, menjünk haza."*

"Come on my darling, let's go home."

As my mother lay in that half-life between this world and the next, I believe God allowed my father to come for her. Taking her hand, he said, *"Gyere drágám, menjünk haza,"* – and he took her home.

Peace, gratitude and a sense of completion washed over me.

My brother arrived, and I left them together. Her forehead was still warm when I kissed her for the last time.

We buried her beside my father, as she had been for over 50 years. Hand in hand. Heart to heart. In the radiant autumn sunshine, the grass wet with rain and the scent of flowers on the breeze, laid to rest in the soft soil of her adopted country she had loved so much.

There was quite a crowd. The ageing Hungarian community – men in dark suits and sombre ties, elegant woman in simple dresses, immaculate jewellery and not a hair out of place. This tiny resilient remnant of Old Hungary. My mother's many Australian friends and all her neighbours.

Two young men turned up looking as if they had just stepped off a building site, their heavy boots incongruous among the well shod. I found out later that they had. Over the past year, they had been renovating a house a few doors down from my mother's. When she discovered there was no running water at the premises, she would regularly take them coffee and biscuits for morning tea.

People from all over Sydney and beyond, from every walk of life came to farewell and honour the shy, unworldly little girl, who had grown into this strong, loving, and much-loved woman. It was the end of an era.

Immediately afterwards I had too much to do to grieve properly. Months later after we sold my childhood home, I took myself off to Russia and spent a week in Tsarskoe Selo. Renamed Pushkin during the Soviet era – Tsarskoe Selo, which means Tsar's Village – is a gracious, elegant town 25 kilometres south of St Petersburg. Since the time of Catherine the Great, Tsarskoe had been the summer retreat of the Romanovs, with its famous blue and gold Catherine Palace as well as the lesser known Alexander Palace, home of the last Tsar and his family. Besotted by imperial Russia since adolescence, Tsarskoe is my favourite place in the entire world. Returning here is the greatest gift I can ever give myself. Sitting in the Alexander Park, the faded ochre walls of the Alexander Palace casting long shadows on the lake, at last I was able to mourn. To remember. And begin to write.

Why did I feel compelled to tell my parents' story?

Because it is not only their story. In many ways it is the saga of all the immigrants who came to Australia in the 1950s and 60s. Those brave, hard-working men and women who arrived here with virtually nothing and went on to forge prosperous, happy, productive lives for themselves and their families. People who proudly called themselves Australian even as they honoured and celebrated their heritage. My parents never stopped being grateful for the opportunities their adopted country afforded him. Dad called himself, "A true blue Aussie-Hungarian. Fate made me Hungarian, but I chose to be Aussie!" he would declare proudly.

And I told it for their granddaughters – Amelia and Angelica. In this increasingly fractured world in which we live, we all need people to look up to and admire. Real people, not the vapid celebrities whose only claim to fame is fame, evidenced by thousands of followers and social media friends.

My parents didn't understand social media and even if they had, they would not have felt compelled to embrace it. The only time I ever heard my mother refer to it, she called it BookFace.

My parents didn't seek virtual friends. They had hundreds of real ones. They didn't aspire to photograph and share every moment of their lives – they just got on with living it to the very best of their ability. They performed no earthshattering deeds, but they made the lives of those who knew them better in myriad small ways. This is what I wanted to share with the two granddaughters who brought such joy to my parents in their later years. This story – heroic in its own simple way and worth remembering. Their legacy worth honouring. Lives lived generously, quietly, honourably.

Their long marriage has been an inspiration. In the beginning there were people who said it was doomed to fail because they were totally incompatible. Came from completely different worlds. And this was true – if it had not been for the disruption of the war and the communist takeover, they would probably never have even met. My father – the city bred, sophisticated, urbane music lover and the innocent wide-eyed country girl. But they did meet and – in the first courageous act of their many courageous acts together – refused the mandatory civil ceremony and found a priest to marry them. Denounced to the authorities by a neighbour, they received an official reprimand and my father was dismissed from his job.

Over the next 50 years, they had their ups and downs, cried and laughed, argued and yelled at each other. My mother slammed pots, pans and doors; my father retreated to listen to Beethoven very loudly until their tempers subsided. But they never went to bed angry. And they never took each other for granted.

As I wrote each chapter of my parents' lives, the past came rushing back to me. The sounds, the scents, the feel of those days.

My father at the piano, playing a complicated Chopin Etude from memory. Each clear and perfect note blending with the background hum of the waves outside.

The sizzle of *Lángos* frying to delicious crispness, ready to be eaten sitting on a Hungarian hillside.

Chocolate hazelnut cake just out of the oven. Rich sweet scents blending with the aroma of strong coffee fresh from the pot.

Apple, sugar and cinnamon wafting through the house as rolls of *rétes* crisp up and brown in the oven.

The gritty trickle of earth falling through my fingers as I sprinkle soil from their garden into my father's grave.

My mother's hands beating egg whites into submission.

I really struggled to complete this final chapter and write about my mother's death. Recalling those terrible days in detail was painful. But it was more than that – I was afraid that once I finished reminiscing about them, my parents would depart from me once more. And having brought them to life years after they died, I could not bear to lose them once again.

But I now realise it doesn't have to be like this. I don't have to lose them. Like the old Hungarian saying, *"Csak az hal meg, akiről nem beszélnek."*

Only he who is not spoken of really dies.

My family will continue to talk about them. Laugh, cry, reminisce about them.

Whenever I attempt one of my mother's recipes, she is here. Struggling to make *beigli* every Christmas and Easter, I feel her standing beside me reminding me that it shouldn't be quite this challenging. "Let me teach you how," she implored while she was alive, and I ignored her. But she shows me now, as I remember how she filled and folded and caressed the pastry.

My niece looks more like my mother with each year that passes. The same thick curling hair, wide forehead and olive skin. More than any of us, Angelica seems to have inherited my mother's culinary skill. She cooks by instinct. Watching her expertly chop onions, I see my mother in her every move. The same quiet competence and determination.

When I listen to the music my father loved and understood so well – he sits beside me. I missed out on my father's musical gifts but inherited his hands – square palms, long slender fingers.

Amelia inherited these too. As well as his quiet wit. And the colour of his eyes, his smile, his mannerisms. Sometimes when she walks away from me, stops suddenly and glances back over her shoulder with a quizzical look – 'Nor I half turn to go yet turning stay[3]', I see my father again.

I know now that their story will live on. Memories, laughter, cherished family recipes, music. Such a rich heritage.

And maybe the most precious legacy of all. The greatest gift a couple can give their children – the knowledge that their parents loved each other deeply, unselfishly to the very end. My father died in my mother's arms. Five years later almost to the day, my mother's last conscious gesture was to put his photo to her lips and kiss it.

Their story is worth telling.

In happier times. John's 21st birthday.
The theme was red and black. And beer!

---

[3] Extract from *Remember*, a poem by Christina Rosetti.

Acknowledgements

This memoir was a long time coming. Life kept getting in the way. But now it's finally here, my grateful thanks to a few of the important people in my life.

Deb – for sharing my memories and helping make some of them.

Sue – whose unfailing wisdom and friendship kept the wheels from falling off my personal chariot more times than I can count.

Justine – my friend and More Than Sister, whose presence in my life is a constant blessing.

James, Emma, Lisa, Lesley and their families – for providing me with myriad opportunity to emulate my mother by cooking gargantuan meals. Food is love – and I love you lots. But it would be wise to continue being nice to me – I may decide to write about you next time.

My brother John – I'm sorry I spent the first 10 years of your life telling everyone mum and dad, "Must have picked up the wrong basket at the maternity hospital!" They didn't – you are a Lang through and through. Resourceful. Resilient. Brave. Slightly insane. This is your story too – I hope you enjoy reliving it.

Angelica – for carrying on our proud culinary tradition, albeit in a vegetarian iteration.

Stuart – for everything. Especially for embracing my crazy, noisy, wonderful Hungarian family and making it your own.

Amelia - I know you 'didn't ask to be born' but I thank God every single day that you were!

And finally – my parents Helen and Otto. I miss you. I love you. I will treasure your memory – forever.

About the Author

After qualifying as a solicitor, Gabriella Lang specialised in litigation for a few years before leaving to work in film and television rights law.

Having seen the error of her ways, she decided to do something useful and in 2006 began to work in philanthropy within the medical research (not-for-profit) sector. She loves learning about all the latest medical breakthroughs and has a firm belief that 'Knowledge is power!' She also thinks it can lead to rampant hypochondria. She continues to fight against it.

Her real passion however, has always been history. Especially Imperial Russian history - something her fiercely patriotic Hungarian father struggled to come to terms with. In spite of his reservations and with his blessing, in 1995, Gabriella embarked on a PhD in Russian history. Her doctoral thesis was titled, *'The Abdication of the Last Tsar. A Reappraisal of the Evidence'*. No-one warned her how challenging it would be to do this while living in Australia – and for this, she is very grateful. Not realising it couldn't be done, she did it. Awarded her doctorate in 2000, this brave (insane?) endeavour necessitated Gabriella living and working in Russia for long periods while conducting research through the archives in Moscow and St Petersburg. She also had to learn to read, write and speak Russian, which made her appreciate that Hungarian is NOT the world's most complicated language.

She has written historical articles for university publications and since 2006, for *Highlife Magazine* and various other publications.

Having travelled extensively throughout Russia and Europe, Gabriella has also written freelance articles for *Weekend Australian Travel and Leisure,* including *Russia's Golden Ring Towns, Hungary – beyond the Tourist Trail,* and *Secrets of St Petersburg.*

In 2017, Gabriella co-authored *The Lost Tutor – John Epps and the Romanovs,* which she wrote with Janet Epps – a relative of John Epps.

In 2018, Gabriella was invited to share her passion for Imperial Russia and teach a course for U3A (University of the Third Age) in the NSW southern highlands. This has now expanded into several courses and includes one on the History of Hungary 1868 – 1956.

Food and Freedom is her first memoir, written to honour and celebrate not only her personal history through her parents' story but also her Hungarian heritage, of which she is immensely proud.

She is working on a second memoir - **Tsars in my Eyes** - about her many trips to Russia, including what it was like doing research in the State Archives in the mid-1990s. At the time. she was the first Australian historian allowed access to the Romanov archive in Moscow.

Married, with a 23-year-old daughter, Gabriella divides her time between Sydney and Bowral in the NSW southern highlands of Australia.

www.ingramcontent.com/pod-product-compliance
Lightning Source LLC
Chambersburg PA
CBHW072049110526
44590CB00018B/3092